The Art
of Buffet
Entertaining

BY Diana and Paul von Welanetz
THE PLEASURE OF YOUR COMPANY (1976)
WITH LOVE FROM YOUR KITCHEN (1976)

The Art of Buffet Entertaining

Diana and Paul von Welanetz

Illustrations by Adrienne Picchi

J.P. Tarcher, Inc.
Los Angeles

Distributed by St. Martin's Press
New York

Design: John Brogna
Manufactured in the United States of America

Published by J. P. Tarcher, Inc.
9110 Sunset Blvd., Los Angeles, Calif. 90069
Published simultaneously in Canada by Macmillan of Canada
70 Bond St., Toronto, Canada M5B 1X3

Our thanks to these publishers and authors who granted permission to include the following: "Brandied Chocolate Fruitcake," from *Valley News*. Reprinted by permission of *Valley News*. "Fresh Nectarine Chutney," from Cecily Brownstone's column. Reprinted by permission of Cecily Brownstone. "Ricotta Macaroon Pie," by Arthur Gold and Robert Fizdale, from *Vogue Magazine*. Reprinted by permission of Arthur Gold and Robert Fizdale. "Black Bottoms Cups" by Harriet Antelyes. Reprinted by permission of Harriet Antelyes. "Camembert Dressing" and "Macadamia Nut Candy" by Kim Dietrich. Reprinted by permission of Kim Dietrich. "Gulliver's Creamed Corn," from Gulliver's Restaurant. Reprinted by permission of Gulliver's Restaurant. "Hazelnut Meringue Torte" by Marlene Sorosky. Reprinted by permission of Marlene Sorosky. "Hot Brie" by Sheila Ricci. Reprinted by permission of Sheila Ricci. "Marinara Dressing" by Mary Swanstrom. Reprinted by permission of Mary Swanstrom. "Pea and Macadamia Nut Salad" by Mildred Mead. Reprinted by permission of Mildred Mead. "Purée of Peas" by Jacques Pépin. Reprinted by permission of Jacques Pépin. " Sunshine Cookies" by Betty Lou Port. Reprinted by permission of Betty Lou Port. "Zucchini Raisin Bread" by Diane Worthington. Reprinted by permission of Diane Worthington. Our thanks also to The Cookstore, L.A.

For Each Other
With The Deepest Love And Respect

Acknowledgments

Our deepest gratitude goes to

Lucy Barajikian, for the love she put into the editing
Alice Blair Simmons for keeping us organized
Our friends who helped us test all the recipes at
our series of buffet parties
Our staff and friends at the von Welanetz Cooking Workshop
at The Cookstore
Jeremy Tarcher and the extraordinary people in his employ

CONTENTS

PREFACE

We love to cook and entertain. For nine years we have been doing both professionally. In addition to running an extraordinarily active cooking school in Los Angeles six days a week, we write a syndicated weekly newspaper food column and are the food editors for an international magazine. We conduct worldwide culinary seminars and have authored two successful cookbooks: *The Pleasure of Your Company,* which won the 1976 Tastemaker Award for Cookbook of the Year in Entertaining, and *With Love From Your Kitchen.*

Even with so much of our time devoted to cooking professionally, we still enjoy entertaining at home. We delight in planning elaborate menus that are easy to prepare and are as tasty and pleasing to our guests as they are gratifying to us. We have found that the buffet is the perfect form for such pleasurable entertaining.

Over the last few years, buffets have grown in popularity, probably because they greatly simplify serving and seating — whether in the most spacious home or the smallest apartment. Yet, many people may hesitate to give a buffet because they are a bit unsure of the planning and coordination involved. We would like to help you take the first step.

As a result, we developed the idea for *The Art of Buffet Entertaining.* In researching and writing the thirteen original menus, we party-tested our recipes with enthusiastic friends. We created the theme of the buffet and prepared the entree ourselves; they prepared the other dishes from our recipes. We then analyzed and criticized our group effort. The results we pass on to you — from warnings about potential surprises to our thoroughly party-tested guidelines for a dazzling success.

INTRODUCTION: WHY A BUFFET?

Our most memorable successes in entertaining have been buffets. Why buffets rather than sit-down dinner parties? The reason is simple: Buffets are a practical and delightful way to entertain any number of guests, in any setting, and for any occasion — from patio to formal dining room, from a Fourth of July barbecue to a black-tie wedding reception. Buffet service is easier for host and hostess and more fun for the guests, seating arrangements are flexible and casual, your friends can mingle freely, and you can enjoy your own party.

This book is your complete guide to the art of buffet entertaining. It takes you from planning to preparing, from serving to after-dinner drinks. In the first part we'll describe how to plan and serve a buffet. You'll learn how to initiate the idea of a buffet, how to set and decorate your buffet table, how to arrange seating for your guests, what to do about serving equipment and help, and how to set up a bar. Serving a buffet includes information on food temperature, placement, traffic flow, and plate clearing. For the most successful and memorable dining affair, we recommend a dress rehearsal. And a party journal will help you keep track of what you did right this time and what not to do next time.

The second part, thirteen original buffet menus, is a script for a buffet from start to finish. The thirteen buffets are set up for convenience of preparation and arrangement. We present a full menu with choices of dishes and a tantalizing rundown of the menu. A description of the table settings and instructions for making and assembling centerpieces for the buffet table and dining table precede a table layout illustration for the food and service. A timetable for presentation several days in advance and a countdown for your last prebuffet hour's work will help you proceed step by step, without last-minute panic.

Recipes for menu items have been standardized to serve multiples of 8, unless otherwise indicated.

A section called Encores at the end of each buffet provides tips on how to use up or store leftovers.

An appendix of Garnishes and Timesaving Techniques will help you put the finishing touches to a picture-perfect buffet.

PART 1.
PLANNING AND SERVING A BUFFET

Even for the most sophisticated partygiver, a buffet requires special care and planning, particularly if it is given for a large number of guests. We have given buffets for years and have encountered almost every conceivable problem that could arise, despite the hours of careful planning we did in advance. In writing this book, then, we have attempted to analyze our successes and some less-than-successes so that we could present you with guidelines for planning and serving buffets and keep the surprises to a minimum. Our aim is to help you give buffets with elegance, grace, and ease—to enhance not only your own pleasure but to delight the eyes and palates of your guests as well.

THE BASIC CONSIDERATIONS FOR PLANNING

The Occasion. The occasion, whether formal or informal, will determine where you hold your buffet, how many guests you invite, and what food you serve.

The Location. Before you center your party around one or several locations, consider how much room you have available. Your ideal party plan may be for a casual buffet. Your guests help themselves to the main course and then step out to the patio or the garden. However, Murphy's Law can prevail: If anything can possibly go wrong, it probably will and at the worst possible moment. This "anything" includes Mother Nature, who, as we all know, has no conscience. And if you've invited fifty guests to a patio party, you may have to crowd them indoors in the event of rain. As long as you have given some

1

thought to the possibility, there is no need for concern. We often set up a tray of hors d'oeuvres in every room of the house, whether we expect rain or not, just to encourage our guests to explore, to thin out, or to find an excuse for a moment away from the madding crowd.

The Guest List. The number of guests you are going to invite will determine the course of your party—seating and serving plans, extra help (if any), and equipment rental, for example. But the important consideration is your guests; you are not planning your guests around your buffet but your buffet around your guests. One of the joys of a buffet is that you can have any number of guests, so go ahead and invite those stimulating people you so often wish to see but to whom you keep postponing an invitation.

At this point you might even consider piggybacking your effort into two parties, one night following another or one luncheon following another. In most cases, if your party is on a Friday, any equipment you rent does not have to be returned until Monday. So with little extra trouble you can usually multiply the do-ahead food and double the pleasures of hospitality.

Once you have your guest list it is time to take pen or telephone in hand. If your buffet is for a formal occasion, you should write the invitations several weeks in advance. Word your invitation so that you receive a definite answer to your RSVP. For less formal occasions, it's desirable to telephone your invitations. You get an immediate yes or no and guests are flattered by the personal attention. However, because nothing is in writing, your guests may not remember the time or date, so be sure to make everything clear—and ask them to write it down.

We have found it useful on written invitations to specify two distinct times: for example, cocktails at 6:00, dinner at 7:00. This announces clearly that your buffet will be served precisely at 7:00. It is unfair to everyone to withhold serving for latecomers. An added advantage is that guests who don't drink can time their arrival for the serving of dinner.

The Menu. The twelve menus in this book are ideal for buffet service. They are easily managed with a minimum amount of equipment, do not require last-minute preparation, and will not suffer if dinner is delayed. They are also delectable. We have chosen the menus for contrasts in flavor (some spicy, some delicate), textures (some crispy, some creamy), temperature (some hot, some cold), and eye-appealing colors. Each menu has been "party tested" in our own home among our friends.

When planning your own buffet menus, keep in mind the same factors that we considered in the planning of this book. Begin your menu by choosing one impressive dish and planning your menu around it. Strive for a harmony of flavors, but take care not to repeat ingredients— all creamy dishes, or all cheesy, herbed, or flavored with sherry. Your ultimate purpose should be to create a menu to please all the senses.

Choose a menu that you feel comfortable preparing. Consider also the cost of the quantity of food and the equipment that you might have to rent, the weather (select your hot or cold menus according to the time of year), the foods in season, the preferences or dietary restrictions of your guests, and the occasion (to provide you with a theme for your buffet).

Buffets lend themselves to any party theme that a sit-down dinner would accommodate, but on a larger scale. Your menu, however, will need to be adapted to the location and the number of guests. For example, it would be difficult to serve precisely timed soufflés or charcoal-broiled steaks if you have 100 guests. It is equally unwise to serve corn-on-the-cob if some of your guests are going to be standing while eating with plate in hand. We have tried to avoid all such problems in the menus we present in this book, though there are a few things you should keep in mind.

1. Meat or other dishes that require knives should be served only at a seated buffet. Serve food that can be eaten with a fork unless you provide tables or lap trays.

2. All main course items are served on one plate, so avoid runny salad dressings or sauces that puddle. Other foods that run or melt might be served in individual ramekins (miniature soufflé dishes) that can be placed right on the plate.

3. Breads and rolls should be prebuttered. French bread should be cut all the way through so that guests can serve themselves easily and eat more comfortably if balancing a plate on their laps.

4. Some buffet foods must be kept hot for at least 30 minutes, so select foods that do not spoil or overcook if kept continuously hot.

PLANNING AHEAD

On the day of a party, you will be putting the kitchen in order, doing last-minute cooking, heating, unmolding, garnishing, dishing up, and finally entertaining your guests. If you do as much as you can as far ahead as you can, you may possibly sidestep Murphy's Law. If nothing can go wrong, nothing will.

When we plan a party our first step is making a checklist. We list every element we can think of, down to the smallest detail, and then sequence our list. We include shopping, rental, delivery, hiring help, decorations, food preparation, setting the tables, serving, and cleaning up, among other items. The list evolves into a day-by-day plan. As we approach the day of the party our countdown becomes hourly.

To help you plan your party, we've included a timetable and countdown for each buffet.

You will develop your own method of checklist planning. After your party, a review and correction of your checklist will give you a "party journal" that will make your next buffet easier to plan.

The Dress Rehearsal. If we could establish one rule for you in the planning of your buffet party, it would be to *go through a buffet rehearsal* with the complete layout of the presentation, including platters, service, and a mock centerpiece. Do this at least a day before your party and take instant-developing snapshots and notes. In the hectic preparty hours you may forget the ideal arrangement you spent hours on. A snapshot will help you instantly recall the balance of your table setting.

Try out recipes before you serve them to your guests. The menus and recipes in this book have been thoroughly party tested; however, don't rule out a mishap or oversight in cooking. The night of your party would be an unfortunate time to find out that you haven't prepared a dish correctly.

DRESSING THE BUFFET TABLE

The purpose of a party is to give you and your friends the opportunity to savor good talk, good food, and good wine. To add to the festive atmosphere, you'll probably want to go to special pains in dressing the buffet table and the dining tables (if you're using them). But you needn't depend on Baccarat crystal, the finest sterling, or priceless family heirlooms to make your table sparkle. (Of course, you can do that if you wish.) Instead, express your own sense of design; forget the formulas and the rules. Your party should reflect your taste and your personality. Today's entertaining is much less formal than it used to be. Your flatware and your plates don't have to match, nor does your linen need to be imported from Ireland. If the table pleases your eye, it's "right."

If you want "expert" advice on color schemes, we suggest that you go to a hobby shop or an artist's supply store and buy an inexpensive color wheel. The wheel will have secondary and complementary color guides to help you select exciting linen combinations. You are the artist and the buffet is your creation. Just turn the wheel to the key color you want to use, for example, yellow-orange. You immediately see through another window its direct harmony contrast, blue-violet—a combination you probably would never have thought of. The important thing is that it be attractive to you.

To help you plan your buffet tables, we have suggested some guidelines on selecting tablecloths, napkins, glasses, china, and silver.

Table Linen. Your tablecloths can set the mood for the entire party. You might follow a color theme such as brilliant oranges, russets, and yellows for Thanksgiving or use a pattern and a small overcloth for another occasion. You might also try a solid color with a center runner for dividing the table into two separate buffet lines. Or, if the main table is really too large for the number of platters, a contrasting center runner can fool the eye into a satisfying sense of compactness.

Since we are both professional and personal partygivers, we take great pride in the total settings for our buffets. But the cost of a variety of table coverings is restrictive, so we have learned to make them ourselves. It's easily and inexpensively done, and we have quickly built up a sizable table dressing wardrobe.

Colored, printed, or white permanent press percale sheets make very handsome and inexpensive tablecloths. Of course, the size of the sheets you buy and their cost will depend on the size of your tables (twin sheets are 66x104 inches; full sheets are 81x104 inches; queen, 90x104 inches; and king, 108x104 inches). Always allow 8 inches all around after hemming for the overhang on dining tables, where people will sit to eat. The buffet table itself should have a cloth that brushes the floor. If you need added length on a cloth, you can stitch on an eyelet ruffle.

Another solution, though slightly more expensive, is to buy drapery or upholstery material. You can buy it in any length and up to 50 or 75 inches in width. (The narrower widths will need to be seamed along the table's edge or down the center, but you'll want to use a runner to hide a center seam.) These fabrics, too, can be a washable permanent press, printed or plain.

You can create shimmering and exquisite color and pattern combinations with the new permanent press fabrics, but they do have minor drawbacks. Most fabrics have a tendency to shrink slightly during the first washing-drying process, so it would be wise to wash, dry, and press your fabric before cutting it or you may discover that your cloth is half an inch shorter the second party around. And unfortunately, the term "permanent press" is misleading. Just before your tablecloths go on your table they need to be well pressed and perhaps perked up with spray sizing. And a final caution: Permanent press fabrics hold stains, especially from red wine.

In addition, we like to spark up our table with the use of contrasting colors in our napkins. If your tablecloth is a solid color, use your eye or your color wheel to select two, four, or six harmonizing colors. If you are using a printed-pattern cloth, select your napkins from one or more of the colors in the print.

We also recommend making your own napkins for the greatest variety. We select the fabric for the color, the print, and the size. The finished product should be at least 20 to 22 inches square with an even hem. So take a piece of paper and pencil with you when you go to a yardage shop to determine how many napkins you can cut from a length of fabric. You can use any scraps to make a few 8½-inch square bottle bibs (napkins that when folded in half and tied around the top of a wine bottle prevent wine spills).

Keep in mind—if you lack patience—that everything from tablecloths and napkins to grass matting can be rented from a party supply. Just check your telephone directory.

Glasses. For a large party we recommend that you rent your glassware. You probably won't have enough of your own, and we've found borrowing to be a poor practice. Rental glassware is inexpensive and comes to you clean, neatly packed in boxes that you can conveniently stack out of sight. Chances are that you won't have a large selection of shapes to choose from, but either the tulip glass or the large long-stemmed bubble glass will suit your purposes perfectly. (We like using large glasses because they need to be filled only half as often.)

For mixed drinks we recommend that you standardize on double-size old-fashioned glasses. We don't suggest using throwaway plastic cups. As convenient as they may be, most are molded of a plastic compound that when mixed with an acidic spirit usually imparts a disagreeable taste to your drink.

China. No one expects you to have thirty place settings of your family china. For a large party you will naturally have to mix-and-match china or rent cups, plates, and bowls from your local party supplier. For smaller gatherings you may wish to invest in an attractive set of party plates. Our beautiful little house restricts our entertaining to twenty-four—twenty-five, if we leave the front door open—so we have selected party plates that we consider to be perfect for buffets. Sometimes referred to as chop plates, they are plain, white, a practical 12½ inches in diameter, and they can hold a lot of food. We think they're well worth the investment.

Serving dishes are most appealing when they vary in size and shape—round, oval, rectangular, or sculptured—and with the exception of very formal buffets, we like to mix and match china, silver, glass, and pottery on our buffet table. Take your menu to your local rental company and select one or two unusual serving pieces with the idea in mind of getting as much height as you can on your table. A high stack of dinnerplates and serving dishes with sculptured edges will give your table a more pleasing third dimension.

Silverware. A party always shines when you use your best flatware. But if you don't have enough settings, you can rent "silverplate" flatware and any other serving equipment. The cost is minimal and the patterns are usually attractive. By going over your menu carefully, you'll know far in advance of your party how many trays, serving pieces, coffee urns, and table settings you will need. Here again we recommend that you not borrow. A spoon chewed up in a disposal can try any friendship, no matter how close.

If we have hired help on the evening of a party, we always stand by two rules: (1) Make certain that sterling flatware with hollow handles and your good silver are never put in the dishwasher; and (2) count the silver to discover whether you have accidentally swept an unseen spoon into the trash.

By the way, camphor or alum kept in your silver chest will prevent tarnishing. Carbon paper works, too.

Centerpieces. If you have a seated buffet, you'll need a small centerpiece for each dining table in addition to the buffet table centerpiece. Each of the buffet menus in this book suggests an appropriate centerpiece and tells you how to assemble it. But the best general guidelines we can offer are to use fresh fruits and vegetables and flowers—all arranged artistically in a bowl or basket. In addition:

1. Don't make your centerpieces or decorations so tall that they obstruct the easy flow of conversation across the table.

2. Combine everything that appeals to you in a composition. You are a better artist than you probably imagine, and in picking fruits and vegetables you have Nature as a helper. Everything she has ever produced combines beautifully in color and shape.

3. If selecting your centerpiece leaves you blank of ideas, look up a recipe—a ratatouille, for example—buy all the ingredients, add a few bunches of parsley, and you have a centerpiece today, Mediterranean vegetable stew tomorrow.

4. You don't have to wash and polish fruits and vegetables. Instead, simply arrange your edibles in a basket, bowl, or on a platter and spray lightly with a nonstick vegetable oil spray (such as Pam, which is nontoxic).

5. If your centerpiece still doesn't look quite right to you and you'd like to have it professionally livened up, take it to your local florist, who can find a few odds and ends to turn it into a masterpiece. Or you can do the job yourself with some flowers from your garden and a handful of inexpensive plastic water tubes from your florist. These water tubes will keep your cut flowers fresh for days. (If you can't find water tubes, place the cut stems in room-temperature water for an hour and then dip them in melted paraffin.)

6. Arrange the centerpieces the day before the party, except for perishable items, which should be added just before the guests arrive.

THE LOCATION AND SETTING
OF THE BUFFET TABLE

It is wise to place your buffet table as near to the kitchen as possible for fast and easy replacement of food. Even if you're giving a patio buffet, there are advantages to serving your buffet from the dining room table next to the kitchen. Depending on how you want your guest traffic to flow and how many dishes you'll have on the buffet table, you have a choice of three standard table locations: against the wall, in the center of the room, or with one main table in the center of the room and duplicate buffets against two walls (useful for especially large parties).

The food that you've attractively arranged on your buffet table is your guests' focal point and your primary decoration. For this reason it should look attractive and appetizing even after your friends have helped themselves. Before a plate on the buffet becomes messy looking or a hot dish gets cold, it should be removed and replaced with a freshly refilled one from the kitchen.

In addition, the food and utensils should be arranged logically on the buffet table. For example, the turkey should be placed before the sauce, in the order that your guests will walk past them. And if there is no one at the table to help serve a dish that requires the use of two utensils, be sure to leave an area next to that dish so that guests may place their dinner plate on the table to free both hands to serve themselves.

These are only very general guidelines. To help you draw your own specific buffet plan, each of the twelve menus in this book has a serving diagram illustrating placement of food on the buffet table. Water, coffee, and tea are generally placed on a side table, and the wine may be served by a helper or placed directly on the dining table for self-service.

SEATING

When it comes to seating your guests, you probably have more entertaining space than you think. Many people happily sit on stairs, lean against walls, perch on pillows, and wander from one room to another seeking new faces. But a rule of thumb for seating your guests is to figure 100 indoor square feet per guest. This means that if your home has 2000 square feet of living space, you can probably seat twenty comfortably. You'll know without question after you've given your first buffet party how many you can easily accommodate.

Consider different types of seating arrangements and experiment to find the one or ones that work for you.

1. *Musical chairs.* The cocktail-and-finger-food buffet, the most casual variety, lends itself to musical chairs seating. Guests are obliged to use only the cushions, chairs, tables, normally available in the room, and when someone gets up, another may quickly preempt the "seat." Young adults seem to cope with this arrangement best.

2. *Casual seating.* Another no-table seating arrangement, casual seating means that you move in chairs from other areas of the house and perhaps conveniently arrange a few small groups of card table chairs. Far from formal, it does give people a fair chance at being comfortable while balancing plates or trays on their knees or eating from individual folding TV tables.

3. *Unassigned table seating.* In our experience, unassigned table seating is the most practical, popular, and informal buffet seating. After serving themselves at the buffet table, your guests may choose their dining companions and sit at a preset table of their choice. (Both tables and chairs can be rented from your local party supplier.)

The easiest way to put this seating into effect is to announce to your guests that dinner is served and that they may pick up a plate at their chosen table and go through the buffet line.

4. *Assigned table seating.* Assigned seating imparts a higher degree of formality to the occasion. Tables are preset and guests look for their names on placecards that designate their seat.

HELP FOR HIRE

The chief advantage of a buffet is that guests can help themselves. Sometimes, however, you could do with some help yourself. Parties may be a labor of love, but any labor is sweeter with a pair of helping hands. You can employ practically any type of service for your party; finding experienced people and being able to afford them are your only considerations. Ask your friends for referrals and check the telephone directory. You can hire musicians, magicians, psychics, handwriting analysts, marionettes, clowns, caricaturists, or even a hunchback doorman with a fright wig for Halloween. To take a more practical point of view, the Yellow Pages offer a rewarding harvest of party suppliers, cooks, bartenders, car parking attendants, cleaning crews, and serving help who will allow you to be guests at your own party.

Caterers. The fee that you pay a caterer is flexible and dependent upon what you ask the caterer to do. The caterer may offer you a package plan for your party or charge you a fixed fee per plate with a guaranteed minimum. Either way the caterer will generally ask and should receive an advance of the fee up to 50 percent. We recommend that the fee be mutually agreed upon and put in writing.

If you are considering putting your party into the hands of a caterer, be certain that the people can handle every aspect; be prepared to discuss everything in detail, from who is to buy the ice cubes to who is to remove the trash at the end of the evening. Some caterers will take every bit of work off your hands that evening and supply everything from food, wine, ice, bartenders, kitchen help, and silver to serving pieces. Others will buy and prepare the food but leave it to you to serve and clean up.

Bartenders. An experienced bartender can be influential in helping you enjoy your own party, since serving drinks can be a time-consuming activity that keeps you away from your guests. If you can afford to hire a bartender, we recommend it as a worthwhile expense.

SETTING UP A BAR AND SERVING WINE

A basic bar should include gin, vodka, light and dark rum, three types of whiskey (scotch, bourbon, and blended for mixed drinks), three selections of wine (Pinot Noir, Chenin Blanc, and Gamay Rosé, for example), dry vermouth, Angostura bitters, medium dry sherry, a good cognac, and a selection of after-dinner liqueurs. Then add to this for the mixes: club soda, tonic, ginger ale, tomato juice, Perrier water for nondrinkers, plenty of ice, maraschino cherries, limes, lemons, a lemon stripper, a cutting board, a sharp knife, water, napkins, glasses, and perhaps a blender. This is by no means a complete list, but it establishes the essentials.

It's always difficult to estimate the number of drinks that will be consumed at a party, but we usually refer to the *Old Mr. Boston Official Bartender's Guide,* which states that for twenty guests at a buffet or dinner, one could expect to serve forty cocktails (3 fifths), fifty highballs (4 fifths), forty glasses of wine (7 bottles), and twenty-five liqueurs (2 fifths). (Note also that an experienced bartender can get twenty drinks from a fifth by using a 1½-ounce jigger.) There are, of course, endless variations on this theme. If you plan on having an open bar, we recommend that you hire an experienced bartender and check your list of the necessary bar stock against his.

For our entertaining, we've standardized on wine and exceptional punches at our parties. The backup of a well-stocked bar, with the exception of vodka and an occasional scotch on the rocks, is rarely needed. Though the wines we serve vary considerably from party to party, according to those we have recently discovered, we almost always have a good white, a good red, and a rosé, with white comprising at least half of our purchase.

We've found that we average 1⅓ bottles of wine per guest through an entire evening, which adds up to 4 bottles for every three guests. We also find it practical to buy wine by the case and take advantage of a 10 percent discount and free delivery.

Chilling wine and champagne for a large party can be a logistical problem; the refrigerator can't hold all of the bottles and buckets are too small. We've settled for an old-fashioned galvanized washtub, still available at hardware stores or easily rented from party suppliers. At least two hours before guests arrive, we fill the tubs with bottles, then blanket the bottles with ice cubes. Be gentle with the champagne, not only in handling but also in chilling—you don't want to lose all of the bubbles in the pop of the cork, nor do you want it to be freezing cold.

KEEPING FOOD HOT

Keeping food hot at a buffet is always a party giver's major concern, but serving from the stove is certainly not the answer. Instead, the following techniques are some effective ways of keeping hot food hot.

First, we suggest that you bring your food directly from stove top or oven to the buffet table at the last minute. If you have no additional heat at the table, use heavy casseroles or earthenware serving pieces, which retain heat longer than other cooking and serving dishes.

If your buffet requires direct heat at the table, you might use an electric warming tray, such as a Salton hot tray, though we prefer independent units, such as a chafing dish with alcohol burner, sterno, or warming candles.

A chafing dish is merely an elaborate double boiler with a heating unit beneath it. If you use an alcohol heating unit, denatured alcohol is the hottest and rubbing alcohol the lowest heat. Sterno is canned heat and gives you approximately the same heat as denatured alcohol; to avoid further cooking, the top of the sterno can has to be adjusted to partially cover the flame and slow down its heating capabilities. Candle-heating units can be bought at your local hardware store; the heat from these candles is too low to bring a cold dish up to serving temperature but it will keep a warm dish warm. Whatever heating unit you choose, be sure to adjust the heat to avoid further cooking your food.

Warm Plates. Next, warm dinner plates will also help keep the food hot. A cold plate will draw heat out of food into itself and will continue to do so until both the plate and the food are the same temperature. To slow down this heat transfer, put as much heat into the plates as your guests can comfortably hold before stacking them on the table. (About 100 degrees is enough to take the chill off.) There are a number of ways to warm plates.

1. If you have the oven space, put your plates in the oven for about an hour with the thermostat set at "warm."

2. Put plates in the dishwasher about a half hour before serving time. Adjust the controls to the drying cycle and leave the plates in.

3. Put plates on an electric hot tray and cover them completely with aluminum foil.

4. Buy an inexpensive Styrofoam picnic ice chest. Place a household heating pad set at "medium" on the bottom. Put your plates on the heating pad, cover them with a bath towel, put the top back on the ice chest and warm the plates for at least 4 hours. If you don't have a heating pad you can heat a brick in the oven, wrap the brick in a towel, and place it in the ice chest with your dishes, once again covering the dishes and the brick with a bath towel and putting the lid on the chest. (The latter is a practical idea for keeping food hot at a picnic.)

5. Electric plate warmers are ideal but rather expensive. They are based on the same principle as a heating pad except that the fabric has pockets in which you place your dishes.

KEEPING FOOD COLD

Your refrigerator is the logical place to chill salad plates or to keep food cold before serving. Put food and plates on the bottom shelf—it's the coldest part of your refrigerator.

As soon as food is removed from an artificially chilled atmosphere to room temperature, it not only offers no resistance but tries as hard as it can to warm up. All you can do is try to delay the warming for as long as possible. There are several ways to keep your food cold.

1. If you have no room in the bottom sections of your refrigerator or freezer, use an ice chest in which you have put a layer of ice cubes covered with heavy aluminum foil. Put plates, bowls, cups, or ramekins, covered with a heavy bath towel, on top of the foil and replace the lid.

If you are placing food in the ice chest, there should be a thicker layer of toweling between the food and the foil-covered ice to prevent either freezing or bruising delicate foods.

2. To keep a bowl chilled at the table, rest it in a nest of crushed ice in a larger bowl. Be sure there is ample room in the larger bowl to contain the water as the ice melts.

3. An alternate method to use if you are going to be short on ice cubes also requires two bowls, one larger than the other. In the bottom of a large bowl place a small packet of Blue Ice. (Blue Ice comes in a sealed plastic bag and when warm, it is pliable like Jello and conforms easily to the bottom of a larger bowl.) Place your second smaller bowl inside the larger bowl on top of the bag of warm Blue Ice, put a weight inside the small bowl, and freeze it all overnight. The Blue Ice will conform to the shape of the bottom and top bowls and can be removed and stored in the freezer until you reassemble for serving.

SERVING A BUFFET AND CLEARING THE PLATES

In all but the most formal buffets, we feel that the host and hostess should be the buffet table helpers. Even if there is no serving to be done, their presence welcomes guests, encourages them to try something new, or assists them when necessary. The host and hostess then serve themselves last.

There are three main styles of buffet service and endless variations.

1. In the first, guests pick up silver, napkins, and plates at the buffet table, serve themselves, and then seat themselves anywhere they wish. After everyone has been served, the buffet table is cleared and reset with desserts and coffee. This plan requires almost no additional

serving help. Its only drawback is that it may prevent slow eaters from going back for seconds or thirds.

2. In an open buffet, a main table, dessert sideboard, and coffee/tea sideboard are continually replenished throughout the evening. Here again, a minimum amount of serving help is required, depending on your menu.

3. In a more formal or elaborate buffet, the first course is placed at preset dining tables before dinner is announced. After the first course the guests are invited to help themselves to the main course at the buffet table. When they leave their seats at the table, the first course dishes are removed by a helper. The procedure of helping oneself from the buffet table is repeated for dessert, concluding with coffee served at the dining table. Maximum serving help is required with this type of buffet.

When you see that everyone's appetite has been satisfied, your next step is to swiftly, dexterously, with as little disturbance to your guests as possible, remove the dirty plates and whisk them out of sight. If you have no kitchen help, you can pile them in the sink and cover them with dish towels. The task of removing plates from the table is best left to your own discretion and available help. But out of sight they must go to make way for the next course, dessert.

We usually handle the transition by mobilizing our available help and announcing dessert, one table at a time. As our guests leave their seats for the buffet table, we quickly repair the damage to their place settings, such as crumbs, ashtrays, or necessary silver, and remove the dirty dishes to the kitchen. We repeat this same process for coffee service.

Now we can take a deep breath, relax, and let our friends and the conversation take over.

MAKING A PARTY JOURNAL

Why throw away the script after you've produced a smash hit? If you keep a party journal, you can give a repeat performance. Make your journal entries the next day; the longer you postpone doing this the more details you will forget. The most valuable part of these notes will be your insights into why something worked so well, why it didn't and what changes you might make next time.

Whatever format you use, we suggest the following entries:

1. *Guest list.* List everyone who was invited and whether by telephone or written invitation. Include a copy of the invitation, if you have

one. If you had an arranged seating plan, make a drawing of who sat next to whom.

2. *Menu.* Describe in detail the party menu and the books in which you found the recipes. Include page numbers or your file card heading. Review and revise your party timetable.

3. *Table diagram.* Draw your buffet table serving arrangement down to the last detail. Label what went in every dish.

4. *Centerpieces and table decorations.* Describe them, including the baskets or containers that held them. Include suggestions for next time. If you've been clever and photographed everything before the guests arrived, you'll have an additional reference when the film comes back from the processor.

5. *Linens and napkin folds.* Recap how you obtained these—bought, rented, or sewn yourself. Would you proceed likewise for your next party?

6. *Party help.* List the name(s) of the help, their phone numbers, what time they arrived, what time they left, what they charged, and your comments.

7. *Rentals.* Enter the name of the rental company, with the phone number and the person who helped you. What did you rent and what did it cost? Would you make any changes next time? Keep the brochure and any receipts with the journal.

8. *Liquor, wine, or punch.* If you used a bartender and didn't list him under party help, write him in here. If you didn't have a bartender, describe the open bar, wines, or punch bowl: what kinds, quantity consumed, quantity remaining, and cost.

9. *After-dinner drinks.* Should you have served them? If you did, what kinds were used and what was the cost?

10. *What did you run short of?* This will be a good reference point for planning your next party's liquor and food requirements.

11. *Comments.* Here you can summarize what you might do next time to forestall any problems or surprises at your next party and you can record your triumphs.

12. *Photos.* If you have taken pictures of the tables before the guests arrived, you will have detailed reminders to refer to. Write the date on the back of each photo and tuck them all into your journal.

The next time you have a buffet, you will be able to learn from your mistakes and duplicate your successes.

Omelette Buffet

Menu

Mimosa Bowl or Bloody Mary Punch

Assorted Fresh Fruit Juices

Choose-Your-Own-Filling Omelettes

Hot Fillings
Flaming Apple
Spanish Sauce
Diced Ham
Crisp Bacon Bits
Sautéed Quartered Mushrooms

Cold Fillings
Caviar
Grated Cheeses
Sliced Scallions
Sour Cream

Cantaloupe Bowls with Fresh Fruit

Zucchini Raisin Bread or
Assorted Danish Pastries

Coffee and Tea

CHOOSE-YOUR-OWN-FILLING OMELETTE BUFFET

An omelette is a cook's best friend: elegant, nutritious, inexpensive, and easy to make. Hosting an omelette buffet is one of the most enjoyable ways to entertain at a Sunday brunch, an informal dinner, or a late supper. It's also fun for the guests because they can become involved in the preparation as they direct you to the fillings of their choice. If they are uncertain, offer your suggestions: The caviar goes well with sour cream and scallions, the Spanish sauce with a cheese omelette. All it takes on your part to become an "eggspert" are a few dozen eggs and some practice.

You can give the party right in your kitchen, or, if you prefer, create the omelette at the buffet table itself. In this case, you will need to rent, borrow, or buy a butane burner—a great gadget for all kinds of showy at-the-table cookery (such as scampi, fettucine, steak "Diana," and crêpes suzettes).

A choice of refreshing punch and fresh fruit juices should be set out on a separate table or sideboard for self-service. The buffet table will hold the omelette fillings, Cantaloupe Bowls, breads, and pastries. Our good friend, Diane Worthington, shared her Zucchini Raisin Bread recipe with us. It's a breeze to make in a food processor but is easily adaptable to a standard electric mixer. A large basket of white and brown eggs—the indispensable ingredient for your omelette making—doubles as a spectacular centerpiece for this "eggs-travaganza" of tastes. No dessert is necessary with brunch, but for evening parties when guests might expect heavier fare, bite-size sweets, such as our recipe for Miniature Strawberry Tarts in the Exotic Curry and Chutney Buffet, would be appropriate.

THE TABLE SETTINGS

This buffet is for any occasion, any time of day or late evening. Fork only is required. Beverages are served separately.

Centerpiece

Buffet Table. Working on the buffet table, place a basket on top of a cake stand and make an arrangement, in pyramid style, of the brown and white eggs you will use in your buffet. Spray the eggs lightly with nonstick cooking spray to give them a sheen. Tuck in small clusters of parsley. The parsley will keep fresh if inserted in water tubes available from your local florist.

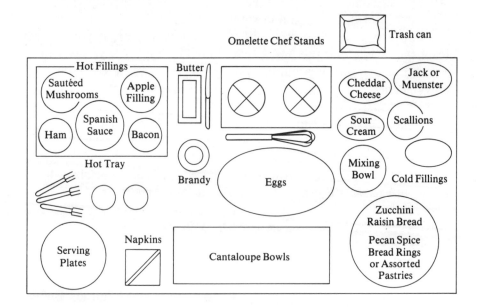

TIMETABLE

Two Days Before the Party. You can prepare the omelette fillings and trimmings and refrigerate them. Grate the cheeses and seal in bottles. Make the Spanish Sauce and apple filling, cool to room temperature, cover, and refrigerate. Bake the Zucchini Raisin Bread, cool, and wrap. Slice the scallions, wrap loosely in a damp paper towel to keep them fresh, and store in a plastic bag in the refrigerator. Cook and drain the bacon, wrap in foil, and refrigerate. Dice the ham and store in a plastic bag in the refrigerator.

The Day Before the Party. Freeze your ice ring. You can save time by premixing the Bloody Mary Punch and storing it, covered, in the refrigerator. Or, if you are serving the Mimosa Bowl, squeeze the orange juice and chill it along with the bottles of champagne. Cut the Cantaloupe Bowls, but leave the seeds in to preserve freshness; cover and refrigerate. Cube the pineapple and dice the oranges; chill them separately, covered with plastic wrap. Prepare the mint sprigs or flowers to garnish the Cantaloupe Bowls and store in the refrigerator. (Wrap the mint sprigs in a damp paper towel inside a plastic bag; place the flowers in a glass of water.)

You can also set up the buffet table with all the serving dishes, hot tray, burners—everything—the day before. Write notes of what goes in each dish and place the notes near the serving dishes. Chill juices in covered serving pitchers. And if your party is to be a Sunday brunch, remember to buy the Danish pastries from the bakery—the store may not be open the day of the buffet; besides, it will avoid a last-minute rush.

The Day of the Party. With all this behind you, you should begin the day of your party with an easy mind. It now becomes a matter of setting out the food: filling the Cantaloupe Bowls with the fruit and adding the garnish, heating a few sauces, finishing the punch, and setting up the centerpiece. Freshen the caviar as directed in the recipe and set it out on the table in a chilled bowl. Sometime before guests arrive, make a practice omelette or two so that you'll feel confident about the procedure.

COUNTDOWN

30 minutes before guests arrive: Recrisp the bacon.
Heat all the hot fillings and place on the hot tray.

	Set out all other ready buffet-table items.
15 minutes before guests arrive:	Unmold the ice ring and finish the punch.
	Prepare tea and coffee.
At serving time:	Place chilled fruit juices on side table.
	Start making omelettes to order.

RECIPES

MIMOSA BOWL

1½ quarts freshly squeezed, strained orange juice, chilled
2 bottles (fifths) dry champagne, chilled

To Serve

Mint Ice Ring or Fern Ice Ring (see Ice Rings in Garnishes appendix)

Just before serving, place the ice ring in a punch bowl. Pour in the orange juice, followed by the champagne. Stir and serve.

BLOODY MARY PUNCH

1½ quarts Snappy Tom or other canned, spicy tomato juice, chilled
1½ cups vodka
¼ cup freshly squeezed, strained lemon juice
1 tablespoon Louisiana red pepper sauce or Tabasco, to taste
¾ teaspoon celery salt
1 teaspoon Worcestershire sauce

To Serve

Cucumber Ice Ring or Lemon Ice Ring (see Ice Rings in Garnishes appendix)
Leafy celery stalks (1 per serving)

Combine the punch ingredients in a punch bowl and mix well. Add the ice ring. Serve over ice cubes in highball glasses with a leafy celery stalk to use as a swizzle stick.

To Prepare in Advance. Combine ingredients, cover, and refrigerate up to 48 hours. Just before serving, stir well and put in punch bowl with ice ring.

CHOOSE-YOUR-OWN-FILLING OMELETTE

Equipment

An omelette pan; a good-sized mixing bowl; a flat, metal, pliable spatula; and for buffet-table cooking, a table-top stove.

The Omelette Pan

The pan you select is a matter of personal choice. We recommend one with a top diameter of 9 to 10 inches (three-egg size). You may find it handy to use a smaller, two-egg size pan with a top diameter of 8 inches. In either case, the only requirement is that it have a flat bottom and sloping sides.

Almost any finish will work well. There is one caution: Never use a Teflon-lined pan for a flambéed omelette; the flames eventually will ruin the nonstick finish. Teflon-lined pans require no special treatment other than a little cooking oil to prevent sticking. All other pans should be reserved for making omelettes (otherwise they will need to be reseasoned with every use) and should not be washed with detergent; simply rinse with plain hot water. If scouring is necessary, pour a little salt in

the pan and heat; remove from heat and rub the stubborn spots with a paper towel.

To Season an Omelette Pan. To season a Teflon pan, wipe a little vegetable oil inside the pan the first time you use it. For other pans, add about 2 tablespoons of vegetable oil, heat in the oven or on top of the range, and with a paper towel rub the hot oil on the inside surface of the pan. Cool to room temperature. Wipe off the excess oil before using. If you reserve your pan for omelette making, you should never have to season it again. Some pans, such as copper ones, have a coating to prevent tarnishing that should be removed according to manufacturer's instructions, then seasoned as directed.

For Each Omelette

3 eggs
1 tablespoon butter or margarine

Break 3 eggs into a mixing bowl (2 eggs may be used for a slightly less impressive looking omelette). Place the omelette pan over medium-high heat. With a whisk, beat the eggs 30 to 40 strokes. When the pan is very hot, drop in 1 tablespoon butter or margarine, and swirl the pan to coat the bottom and sides. When the butter has melted, pour in the eggs.

Stir the eggs slowly with the end of a flat, metal spatula until the egg starts cooking. Now, while shaking the pan gently in a circular fashion, lift the edges of the omelette with the spatula to allow the uncooked egg to run underneath. (The action is somewhat like sweeping dust under a rug.) Avoid the tendency to pull the cooked part toward the center of the pan while you lift the edges or your omelette will be thick in the center. Keep the pan on the heat so that the cooking stays constant. When the egg is firm, reduce the heat and add about ¼ cup of the desired filling(s) in a strip down the center or on one half of the omelette. Use the spatula to fold the other half over the filling. If a guest wants a lightly browned omelette, leave it in the pan for a few seconds longer after folding.

To remove the omelette from the pan, shake it gently to make sure it is loose. This will pose no problem if your pan has been properly seasoned and you have not skimped on the butter. The most dramatic way to turn out an omelette is to hold the warm serving plate in your left hand (left-handed cooks, use your right hand), swing the pan up in an arc and invert the omelette on the plate. This takes practice and a little courage. The most sensible method is to shake the omelette to the edge of the pan and simply slide it out or turn it over carefully onto the serving plate. If you are uneasy about your technique—most people are—practice on family or friends so that on the day of your buffet your guests dine on moist and puffy omelettes.

FLAMING APPLE OMELETTE
For 4 omelettes

The Filling
  1 (24-ounce) jar chunky-style applesauce
  1 tablespoon sugar
  1 teaspoon ground cinnamon
  2 tablespoons fresh lemon juice
  Zest (yellow peel) of 1 lemon, finely chopped

To Serve
  Cognac or brandy to flambé the omelette
  ¼ cup sour cream per omelette

Combine the filling ingredients in a small heavy saucepan. Bring to a boil over low heat and simmer for 1 or 2 minutes to dissolve the sugar.

Make the omelette as described; use the apple mixture as a filling. (*Caution:* Do not use a Teflon-lined pan. Flambéing the omelette will ruin the finish.) Fold the omelette and remove the pan from the heat. Heat the cognac or brandy in a ladle until hot and ignite it with a match. Hold the pan away from you and quickly pour the flaming liquid over the omelette. Move your hand away immediately to avoid the high flames that result when the liquid is ladled into the pan. Shake the pan gently until the flames die down. Turn the omelette out on a serving plate and top with a dollop of sour cream.

To Prepare in Advance. Refrigerate the filling up to a week. Heat before using.

SPANISH SAUCE
For 4 omelettes

2 tablespoons butter or margarine
2 tablespoons olive oil
2 green peppers, cut into ¾-inch pieces
2 medium onions, coarsely chopped
16 medium fresh mushrooms, cleaned and cut
    in quarters through the stems
1 (1-pound, 14-ounce) can solid-pack tomatoes,
    with liquid (see *Note*)
1 medium clove garlic, pressed
2 teaspoons salt
¾ to 1 teaspoon freshly ground black pepper
Tabasco sauce or cayenne pepper,
    to taste (optional)

Note: Tomatoes packed in tomato purée are best for most sauces.

Melt the butter or margarine with the olive oil in a large skillet over medium heat. Sauté the green pepper and onions for a few minutes until the onions are transparent. Stir in the mushrooms, tomatoes, garlic, and seasonings. Simmer, uncovered, about 10 minutes, or until the sauce is slightly thickened.

To Prepare in Advance. The sauce can be made up to two days before. Cool and store in the refrigerator. Reheat gently before serving, taking care not to overcook the mushrooms.

DICED HAM
For 4 omelettes

½ pound fully cooked ham, diced

To Prepare in Advance. The diced ham can be stored in a plastic bag in the refrigerator up to five days.

CRISP BACON BITS
For up to 8 omelettes

½ pound regular or thick-sliced bacon

There are two methods for making bacon bits. The easiest way is to cut the strips crosswise into ¼- to ½-inch strips and fry them in a large skillet until rendered and crisp. Drain on paper towels. The more traditional method is to cook the bacon strips whole, drain, then crumble. Serve warm in a bowl with a spoon for sprinkling. For up to 8 omelettes.

To Prepare in Advance. The bacon can be cooked up to a week in advance by either method. Drain, cool, and refrigerate, wrapped in foil. Heat uncovered in a 350° oven about 5 minutes to recrisp.

SAUTÉED QUARTERED MUSHROOMS
For 4 omelettes

2 tablespoons butter or margarine
2 shallots, minced
1½ pounds fresh mushrooms, cleaned and cut in
  quarters through the stems
1 cup dry white wine
1 tablespoon fresh lemon juice
1 tablespoon minced parsley
Salt and freshly ground pepper, to taste

Melt the butter or margarine in a large skillet over medium heat. Sauté the shallots for a few seconds, taking care not to burn them, add the mushrooms, and toss to coat. Pour in the wine and lemon juice. Simmer over high heat until most of the liquid has evaporated. Add parsley, salt, and pepper. Taste and adjust seasoning. Remove from heat and serve promptly.

To Prepare in Advance. For best flavor and texture, the mushrooms should be served immediately. If they must stand for a while, they will soften slightly and release more liquid, but the flavor will still be piquant.

CAVIAR
For 4 omelettes

4 to 8 ounces lumpfish caviar (available in jars)

To Serve
Sour cream
Thinly sliced scallions

Place the caviar in a fine mesh strainer. Rinse under slow-running cold water to remove all traces of the black inky liquid. Turn out gently on paper towels to dry. Behold: miniature black pearls, now so much more appetizing in flavor and appearance! Serve in a shell or small dish with a "caviar shovel" or mother-of-pearl serving spoon. Fill the omelette with a small spoonful of caviar, a dollop of sour cream, and a sprinkling of scallions.

To Prepare in Advance. Place the prepared caviar in its serving dish, cover with a damp paper towel. Chill up to 6 hours.

GRATED CHEESES
For up to 16 omelettes

½ pound sharp Cheddar cheese
½ pound Muenster or Monterey Jack cheese

Grate the cheeses (use a food processor if you have one for grated cheese in a flash) and place in separate bowls for serving.
To Prepare in Advance. The cheeses can be grated, gently placed in jars to prevent crushing, and chilled up to two or three days. For best flavor, remove from refrigerator at least 1 hour before serving.

SLICED SCALLIONS
For up to 16 omelettes

2 bunches scallions

Cut the scallions crosswise in thin slices. Serve in a bowl with a spoon for sprinkling.

To Prepare in Advance. The scallions can be sliced, wrapped loosely in a damp paper towel, and stored in a plastic bag up to two days before the buffet.

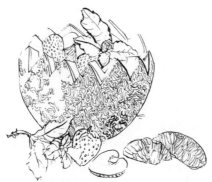

CANTALOUPE BOWLS WITH FRESH FRUIT
4 small ripe cantaloupes
3 cups (1 box) fresh strawberries
½ fresh pineapple, cut in chunks
2 oranges, peeled, white membrane removed, diced, and seeded
1 tablespoon orange liqueur or brandy (optional)

The Garnish
8 sprigs mint or flowers (daisies or bougainvillaea)

Cut cantaloupes in half and zigzag the edges with a sharp knife. Scoop out the seeds. Cut a thin slice off the bottom of each half so that it will sit firmly without wobbling. Rinse the strawberries, hull, and dry them on paper towels. If they are large, cut them in half. Set aside. Combine the orange and pineapple pieces in a refrigerator bowl. Toss with the orange liqueur or brandy and refrigerate until needed.

Within 2 hours of serving, combine the strawberries and the pineapple-orange mixture and fill the centers of the cantaloupes. Arrange the halves on a serving tray large enough to hold them all, or use two trays if they will not fit on one. Garnish each cantaloupe bowl with a sprig of mint or a fresh flower.

To Prepare in Advance. The Cantaloupe Bowls can be cut the day before, but leave the seeds in to preserve freshness. Cover with plastic wrap and store in the refrigerator. At the same time, cube the pineapple and dice the oranges; store them separately in the refrigerator covered with plastic wrap. Combine them with the liqueured fruit within 2 hours of serving. Discard the cantaloupe seeds, fill the cavities with the fruit chunks, and garnish.

ZUCCHINI RAISIN BREAD

2 cups shredded zucchini (2 small or 1½ medium)
2 eggs
1 cup sugar
½ cup vegetable oil
1½ teaspoons vanilla extract
1½ cups all-purpose or whole wheat flour
1½ teaspoons ground cinnamon
½ teaspoon salt
½ teaspoon baking soda
¼ teaspoon baking powder
½ cup walnut pieces
½ cup raisins or dried currants

Grease and flour a 9x5x3-inch loaf pan. Preheat the oven to 350°.

To Make in a Food Processor. Attach the shredder disk in the food processor and shred the zucchini to make exactly 2 cups. (To facilitate its fitting into the feed tube, cut the zucchini in half crosswise and lengthwise, then stand the pieces upward in the feed tube.)

Replace the shredder disk with the plastic blade (no need to wash the processor bowl) and add the eggs. Process a few seconds until frothy, then add the sugar, oil, and vanilla and process until the mixture is thick and lemon colored.

Sift together the flour, cinnamon, salt, baking soda, and baking powder. Add them to the bowl and turn the motor on and off quickly two or three times until blended. Repeat this process with the nuts and raisins or currants.

Pour the batter into the loaf pan. Bake for 60 to 70 minutes or until the bread feels firm in the center when pressed with your fingertips or a cake tester comes out clean. Cool the loaf in the pan for 20 minutes, then invert onto a rack to cool completely. The bread is delicious served warm or cold.

To Make with an Electric Mixer. Use a medium shredder to grate the zucchini. In the large bowl of the mixer, beat the eggs until frothy. Add the sugar, oil, and vanilla and beat until light and lemon colored. Sift the flour, cinnamon, salt, baking soda, and baking powder together and beat them slowly into the wet ingredients. Fold in the nuts and raisins or currants. Bake as directed in the processor method.

To Prepare in Advance. When wrapped airtight, the loaf can be stored at room temperature up to three days, in the refrigerator for at least a week, or in the freezer up to three months.

ENCORES

While you're cleaning up, you'd best polish off the caviar and the Mimosa Bowl—not an unpleasant task! Funnel the Bloody Mary Punch or leftover juices into a bottle for refrigerator storage of up to a week. All the omelette fillings and sauces will keep in the refrigerator for several days, ready when you are for an instant family brunch or supper. The pastries and breads can be frozen for another day. When ready to use, simply thaw and reheat, either in a conventional oven or a microwave oven.

Make-Your-Own-Salad Buffet

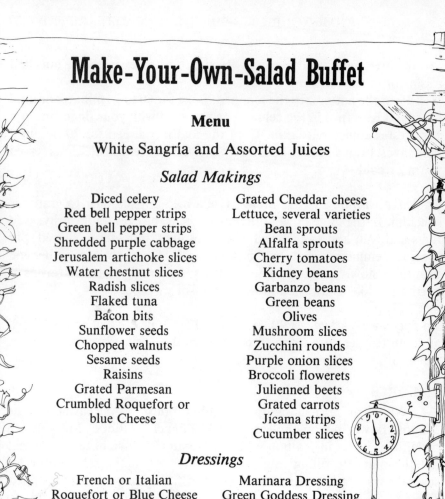

Menu

White Sangría and Assorted Juices

Salad Makings

Diced celery	Grated Cheddar cheese
Red bell pepper strips	Lettuce, several varieties
Green bell pepper strips	Bean sprouts
Shredded purple cabbage	Alfalfa sprouts
Jerusalem artichoke slices	Cherry tomatoes
Water chestnut slices	Kidney beans
Radish slices	Garbanzo beans
Flaked tuna	Green beans
Bacon bits	Olives
Sunflower seeds	Mushroom slices
Chopped walnuts	Zucchini rounds
Sesame seeds	Purple onion slices
Raisins	Broccoli flowerets
Grated Parmesan	Julienned beets
Crumbled Roquefort or	Grated carrots
blue Cheese	Jícama strips
	Cucumber slices

Dressings

French or Italian	Marinara Dressing
Roquefort or Blue Cheese	Green Goddess Dressing
Thousand Island	Tomato Herbal Dressing
Sherry Cream Dressing	Marjorie's Dressing

Rolls, Crackers, Bran Muffins or Zucchini Raisin Bread

Triple Chocolate Cheesecake

THE 40-INGREDIENT, MAKE-YOUR-OWN-SALAD BUFFET

When guests see our salad bar, eyes light up. A salad bar is almost sinfully fun—and heathy, with its mountain of salad makings and assorted dressings and toppings.

Naturally, the attraction of this light buffet is the food itself. The mounded, chopped, diced, and shredded vegetables rival an artist's palette. Along with the salad bar, arrange a serve-yourself bar of assorted fruit juices for guests to mix their own combinations—with perhaps a bottle of vodka discreetly placed for anyone who may wish to spike the juice—or offer White Sangria.

The Sherry Cream Dressing has proven popular with oenophiles (wine lovers) because the sherry doesn't fight with the wine being served. The Marinara Dressing is a very zippy addition and comes to us via our friend, Mary Swanstrom. It is also delicious served with mixed greens, garnished with tiny shrimp, or when spooned over sliced fresh tomatoes. The Green Goddess dressing originated at the Garden Court of the Sheraton-Palace Hotel in San Francisco to honor the opening of the play, *The Green Goddess*. Our version is also great as a dip for crudités (cut fresh vegetables) or crisp-cooked broccoli. As for the Tomato Herbal Dressing, it is our creation, made especially for those who need to watch their weight.

For dessert there is an elegant cheesecake with a surprisingly light and creamy, mousselike filling. It's truly spectacular, made more so when decorated with a cloud of powdered sugar and chocolate curls. The White Sangria appears in the Creamy Cannelloni or Quiche Luncheon Buffet. Marjorie's Dressing appears in the Elegant Open House Buffet and the Zucchini Raisin Bread in the Choose-Your-Own-Filling Omelette Buffet.

31

THE TABLE SETTINGS

This is a lavish, but casual, single-line buffet. Fork only is required. Beverages and dessert are served separately.

Centerpiece

Buffet Table. From your local nursery, buy a selection of inexpensive seed packets with full-color pictures on them of lettuce, tomatoes, and green beans. Empty the packets of their contents (preferably in your garden), mount the envelopes on bamboo skewers, spear the skewers into plump tomatoes or tiny flowerpots filled with raw beans, and place them among the salad makings.

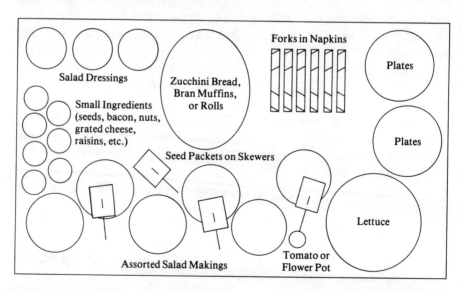

TIMETABLE

Two Days Before the Party. Make all the dressings ahead—it improves their flavor. Bake the Zucchini Raisin Bread and wrap it airtight. Make the Triple Chocolate Cheesecake and chocolate curls.

The Day Before the Party. Grate the cheeses and refrigerate in jars to prevent crushing. Prepare the bacon bits. Buy the fruit juices. We suggest a health food store for their variety. Set out everything necessary for a serve-yourself juice bar—ice bucket and tongs, glasses, cocktail napkins. Or, if serving White Sangría in a punch bowl, freeze your ice ring and combine the wine mixture and chill.

Up to 8 Hours Before the Party. All the fresh vegetables can be washed, dried, and stored in serving bowls inside plastic bags. Set out nuts, seeds, and other nonperishable items on the serving table. Slice the Zucchini Raisin Bread, arrange on a serving plate, and cover with a damp towel, or place rolls, muffins or crackers in a basket.

COUNTDOWN

1 hour before guests arrive:	Place salad dressings on buffet to come to room temperature. Garnish cheesecake and chill.
15 minutes before guests arrive:	Set out pitchers of juices and ice cubes. Unmold ice ring and place in punch bowl. Set out all salad ingredients and bread.
As guests arrive:	Add champagne and grapes to White Sangría mixture.

RECIPES

SALAD MAKINGS

You will have to be the judge of the amounts here because they will depend entirely on the number of different items you decide to have. Of course, the larger the array, the more beautiful your salad bar. Best of all, leftover ingredients will keep to give you other "salad days."

Just a word about lettuce: There are infinite varieties in the market. Depending on the number of guests you invite, why not plan to use several kinds? Don't forget watercress, spinach, and escarole. They make congenial additions to your other crisp, fresh greens.

SHERRY CREAM DRESSING
For 2 cups, or about 8 servings

¼ cup red or white wine vinegar
1 small clove garlic, pressed
1 egg yolk
1 teaspoon salt
¼ teaspoon sugar
1⅓ cups salad oil
⅔ cup olive oil
¼ cup dry or medium-dry sherry
½ teaspoon celery seed

For 16 Servings. Recipe can be doubled if using an electric mixer. Some blenders will not hold a double recipe.

For 32 Servings. A triple recipe, made in two batches, should be sufficient.

In a blender or the large bowl of an electric mixer, combine the wine vinegar, garlic, egg yolk, salt, and sugar. Blend until thoroughly combined and creamy. Beat in the oils in a slow steady stream while the motor is running. Add the sherry in a slow steady stream. Stir in the celery seed. Taste and adjust the seasonings. For best flavor, serve at room temperature.

To Prepare in Advance. This will keep for several weeks in the refrigerator. Do not freeze. For best flavor, bring to room temperature before serving.

MARINARA DRESSING
For 1½ cups, or about 8 servings

1 (2-ounce) can anchovy fillets, drained, or 1 tablespoon anchovy paste
1 tablespoon freshly squeezed lemon juice

4 teaspoons minced chives
2 medium cloves garlic, pressed
Several dashes Worcestershire sauce
½ teaspoon dry mustard
½ teaspoon paprika
½ teaspoon freshly ground black pepper
1 cup olive oil
¼ cup red wine vinegar

For 32 Servings. A triple recipe should be sufficient.

In a mixing bowl mash the anchovies with the lemon juice, chives, garlic, Worcestershire sauce, mustard, paprika, and pepper. Slowly whisk in the oil and wine vinegar. Cover and let stand at room temperature for at least 1 hour before serving to allow the flavors to blend. Taste and adjust the seasonings before serving.

To Prepare in Advance. Store in the refrigerator up to one week. For best flavor, bring to room temperature before serving.

GREEN GODDESS DRESSING
For 1 quart, or about 16 servings.

2052915

1 scallion
1 bunch fresh chives
½ cup firmly packed parsley leaves
1 small clove garlic, pressed (optional)
8 anchovy fillets from a 2-ounce can, drained and minced, or 2
    teaspoons anchovy paste
2 tablespoons fresh tarragon leaves, or 2 teaspoons dried tarragon
2 teaspoons Dijon-style mustard (preferably Poupon label)
¼ cup white wine vinegar or tarragon vinegar
2½ cups mayonnaise
½ cup sour cream

To Make the Dressing in a Mixing Bowl. Finely chop the scallion, chives, and parsley. Combine in a mixing bowl with the remaining ingredients and mix thoroughly.

To Make the Dressing in a Food Processor. Process the scallion, chives (cut in small sections), parsley, garlic, anchovy, and tarragon briefly with the steel blade. Change to the pastic blade and add the remaining ingredients, processing just until well blended.

Cover and refrigerate at least 2 hours to mellow flavors. Taste and adjust seasonings. Serve at room temperature.

To Prepare in Advance. The dressing can be stored in the refrigerator up to one week. For best flavor, bring to room temperature before serving.

TOMATO HERBAL SALAD DRESSING
For 1½ cups, or 8 servings

> 1 cup tomato-vegetable juice (preferably V-8 brand)
> ¼ cup red wine vinegar
> ½ teaspoon sugar
> ¼ teaspoon ground cumin
> ¼ teaspoon dried oregano, crumbled
> ¼ teaspoon celery salt
> 1 medium clove garlic, pressed
> ⅛ teaspoon freshly ground black pepper
> Dash Worcestershire sauce
> 2 teaspoons cornstarch
> 2 tablespoons cold water
> 2 tablespoons minced chives
> 1 tablespoon olive oil or vegetable oil

In a small saucepan, bring to a simmer the tomato-vegetable juice, wine vinegar, sugar, cumin, oregano, celery salt, garlic, pepper, and Worcestershire sauce. Stir the cornstarch into the water until dissolved, then stir it into the dressing until thickened. Remove from heat and cool. Stir in the chives and oil. Cool and adjust seasonings to taste. Serve at room temperature for best flavor.

To Prepare in Advance. This dressing will keep indefinitely in a covered container in the refrigerator. For best flavor, serve at room temperature.

TRIPLE CHOCOLATE CHEESECAKE
For up to 16 servings

The Crust

> 1 (8½-ounce) package Nabisco Famous Chocolate Wafers
> ¼ pound (1 stick) butter or margarine, softened or melted

The Filling

    3 large eggs
    1 cup sugar
    3 packages (8 ounces *each*) cream cheese, at room temperature
    12 ounces (3 bars) Baker's German Sweet Chocolate
    ⅓ cup dark rum (preferably Myer's label)
    5 teaspoons instant coffee powder or granules
    2 teaspoons vanilla extract
    ⅛ teaspoon salt
    1 cup (½ pint) sour cream

The Garnish

    Powdered sugar
    Chocolate curls (recipe follows)

To make the crust, crumb the chocolate wafers in a blender or food processor, processing one third of the cookies at a time. Combine the crumbs with the softened or melted butter or margarine and pat the mixture into the bottom and up the sides of a 9-inch spring-form pan to within ¾ inch of the top rim. Refrigerate the crust while you prepare the filling.

Preheat the oven to 350°. In a large mixing bowl beat the eggs with the sugar until light and lemon colored. Beat the cream cheese until the mixture is very smooth. Set aside. Melt the chocolate with the rum, coffee, vanilla, and salt in the top of a double boiler placed over barely simmering water. Stir until the chocolate is dissolved. Beat the warm chocolate mixture into the cream cheese mixture. When well blended, beat in the sour cream, mixing thoroughly. Pour the filling into the crumb crust. Place a piece of aluminum foil about 12 inches square under the spring-form pan and bring the sides of the foil up around the pan. The foil will catch the butter that will leak from the crust during baking.

Bake for 1 hour at 350° or until the cheesecake feels firm when pressed with your fingertip one inch from the center. The cake will continue to bake when removed from the oven. Cool on a rack at room temperature, then refrigerate for at least 6 hours before cutting. Serve chilled.

To garnish the cheesecake, dust powdered sugar heavily over the top by pressing it through a kitchen strainer with the back of a spoon. Top with chocolate curls. To facilitate cutting, dip serving knife in warm water after each slice.

To Prepare in Advance. The cake can be baked at least two days before serving. Decorate within 6 hours of serving and keep chilled.

Afterthought. This dessert can be transported very easily to another home if you leave the spring-form sides of the pan in place and wrap the cake in several layers of foil.

CHOCOLATE CURLS

4 ounces semi-sweet or Baker's German's Sweet chocolate
½ teaspoon vegetable oil

Melt the chocolate in the top of a double boiler over hot, not boiling, water. Stir constantly until the chocolate is melted. Remove from heat and stir in the oil. Pour the blended mixture into a 3½-ounce disposable plastic cup (preferably Solo brand) to cool. Chill.

Remove the cup from the refrigerator about half an hour before working on it. Remove the chocolate from the cup. To prevent the heat of your hands from melting the chocolate hold it with a towel on the two ends. With a vegetable peeler shave down the side from the small end toward the large end. The cut chocolate will roll and "curl." Drop each curl onto a cold plate, and keeping the chocolate chilled, make as many curls as you need.

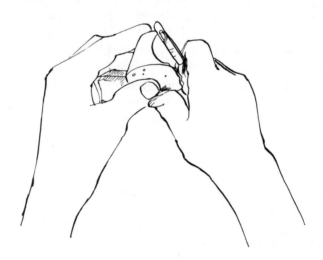

To Prepare in Advance. Store in an airtight container in the refrigerator up to three days. Or, freeze for a week, carefully wrapped to prevent breakage. If stored longer, the curls will cloud and turn white.

ENCORES

The Sangría will lose its sparkle and be diluted from the ice, but if you have a considerable amount left over you won't want to throw it down the drain. Instead, put back flavor with more orange liqueur and sparkle with fresh champagne or club soda.

The salad fixings will keep for a week and make delightful nibbles for luncheon or dinner salads if you freshen the vegetables in an hour-long ice bath, then drain, wrap in paper towels, and refrigerate in plastic bags ready for use. If there is an excess of vegetables, toss some in a pot, add water to cover, sprinkle of seasonings, and create your own vegetable soup. A favorite one at our house is full of cabbage, bell peppers, carrots, celery, and a touch of garlic.

The cheesecake will keep for you to enjoy another day. Wrap any leftover zucchini bread airtight, then store in the refrigerator or freezer to slice thinly for tea sandwiches filled with cream cheese.

CANNELLONI or QUICHE LUNCHEON BUFFET

Menu

White Sangría or Lillet

Spinach Cannelloni Mornay
or
Quiche von Welanetz

Minted Fruit Cups
or
Magical Mangoes

Herbed Pita Rounds

Iced Strawberry Soufflé
with
Chocolate-Dipped Strawberries

Coffee and Tea

CREAMY CANNELLONI OR QUICHE LUNCHEON BUFFET

Numerous occasions throughout the year call for the serving of a light lunch: charity meetings, bridal showers, bridge clubs, informal after-church gatherings, or no-reason-at-all-but-do-let's-meet affairs. The uncomplicated versatility of this menu is perfect for such days. You have a choice of two refreshing fruited drinks: White Sangría or our favorite apéritif, Lillet (pronounced lee-*lay*), made from white wine and brandy and flavored with herbs. If serving Lillet, do so only before lunch, then serve wine with the main course.

We discovered the spinach-stuffed cannelloni at the Del Prado restaurant in Mexico City and could hardly wait to create our own recipe at home. Both the cannelloni and the 3-inch-high elegant quiche can easily be prepared ahead of time. In fact, advance preparation gives flavors a chance to blend and improve. The wide variety of fresh fruits offered in our markets makes the Minted Fruit Cups capable of infinite variations. We serve them in miniature soufflé dishes (3- to 4-ounce capacity). This is an ideal way to serve any "wet" items (sherbets or salads, too) to prevent liquids from seeping into other foods on the serving plates.

Pita bread, also known as pocket bread, is used for our Herbed Pita Rounds. We toast them crisp and they are redolent with herbed butter.

We practiced a minor deception in naming the dessert. Although Iced Strawberry Soufflé has the appearance of a soufflé, it is actually a mousse. If fresh or frozen strawberries are not available, you may substitute another light dessert such as our Iced Margarita Soufflé, which appears in the Mexican Fiesta Buffet. The recipe for Magical Mangoes appears in the Garnishes appendix.

THE TABLE SETTINGS

This is a simple luncheon buffet for which fork and spoon are required. Wine, dessert, and beverages are served separately.

Centerpieces

Buffet and Dining Tables. For each centerpiece, crowd bunches of parsley in an upright position into containers of water fitted into a basket or flowerpot. Cut the parsley stems so that the center of the arrangement is higher in the middle. Stud with an assortment of non-toxic flowers (such as roses, daisies, bachelor's buttons) to make an attractive arrangement. Be sure the flower stems reach the water. Centerpieces can be prepared 8 hours in advance if you spray them with a mister and cover them loosely with a damp tea towel. Store in a cool, dark place.

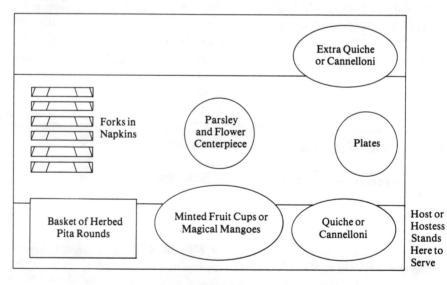

TIMETABLE

Two Days Before the Party. The advantage of choosing Spinach Cannelloni Mornay as the main course is that it can be made at your convenience, assembled in an oven-to-table serving dish, and refrigerated (or it may be frozen up to two months in advance). It requires only overnight thawing and last-minute baking on the day of the luncheon.

The Day Before the Party. Quiche von Welanetz must be serve within 24 hours after preparation. If you keep some frozen quiche shells on hand for convenience, as we do, you need prepare only the filling the day before the party, pour it into the shells, and bake before going to bed. Cool on racks at room temperature. You can also make the Iced Strawberry Soufflé the day before. Chill the Lillet or the component parts of the White Sangría. Freeze your ice ring, if serving the Sangría.

On the Day of the Party. Arrange the individual salads or mangoes on a serving plate, cover with a damp tea towel, and store in the refrigerator. Dip the strawberries into the melted chocolate and keep chilled. Butter and season the pita rounds for last-minute toasting in the same oven in which you have the cannelloni or quiche baking. Cut the oranges or limes into thin slices for the drinks, and cover with plastic wrap until serving time.

COUNTDOWN

30 minutes before guests arrive:	Remove cannelloni from refrigerator or cut quiche into serving pieces and place on baking sheet.
15 minutes before guests arrive:	Preheat over to 350°.
	Unmold ice ring and place in punch bowl with White Sangría ingredients, except champagne; or if serving Lillet, place orange slices in wineglasses.
	Prepare coffee and tea.
As guests arrive:	Add champagne to punch bowl for Sangría or pour Lillet into wineglasses.

25 minutes before serving:	Bake cannelloni for 20 minutes.
	or
15 minutes before serving:	Bake quiche slices for 10 minutes.
10 minutes before serving:	Bake pita rounds for 7 to 10 minutes. Warm serving plate for bread.
5 minutes before serving:	Place tray of salads or mangoes on buffet table. Garnish and set out hot foods. Announce lunch.
Just before serving dessert:	Remove collar from the soufflé and garnish.

RECIPES

WHITE SANGRÍA

    1 bottle (fifth) white Chablis
    ½ cup orange liqueur (Triple Sec, Cointreau, or Curacao)
    4 limes, thinly sliced

To Serve

    8 small bunches green seedless grapes
    1 bottle (fifth) champagne, chilled
    Mint Ice Ring or Lime Ice Ring (See Ice Rings in Garnishes appendix)

Combine Chablis, orange liqueur, and sliced limes in a pitcher and chill thoroughly. To serve, pour into a punch bowl; add the grapes, champagne, and ice ring. Or, omit the ice ring and serve in a pitcher.

To Prepare in Advance. The wine mixture can be chilled up to three days. Proceed as directed when ready to serve.

LILLET

    1 bottle (fifth) Lillet, chilled
    8 thin orange slices

Slice the oranges early in the day and reassemble into their original shape. Cover with a damp paper towel and refrigerate until serving time. To serve, place orange slices in well-chilled, large wineglasses and pour in the well-chilled Lillet.

SPINACH CANNELLONI MORNAY
For 16 cannelloni (8 to 16 servings)

16 five-inch crêpes (recipe follows)

3 pounds fresh spinach leaves, stemmed and finely chopped, or 3 (10-ounce) packages frozen chopped spinach, thawed and squeezed of all excess moisture
¼ pound (1 stick) butter or margarine
1 tablespoon olive oil or vegetable oil
2 medium onions, minced
3 medium cloves garlic, pressed
½ cup all-purpose flour
4 cups milk
2 teaspoons celery salt
Salt, to taste
½ teaspoon freshly ground black pepper
A pinch of thyme
¼ teaspoon freshly grated nutmeg
½ cup freshly grated Parmesan cheese
¼ teaspoon white pepper, or a good dash of cayenne pepper
1 tablespoon butter
2 tablespoons minced parsley

Prepare the crêpes according to the directions, or, if frozen, return to room temperature before attempting to separate them.

If using fresh spinach, wash and place it, without additional water, into a pan, cover and cook for 6 minutes. When cool, squeeze out excess liquid. Set aside.

In a large skillet, melt the butter with the oil. Sauté the onions and garlic over medium heat about 5 minutes until the onions are transparent. Stir in the flour and cook slowly for a few minutes, stirring constantly, until the raw taste is gone. Remove the pan from the heat, gradually stir in the milk, and add the celery salt. Return to heat and stir the mixture over medium heat until it is thickened and bubbly. Remove from heat. Taste and season with salt, if necessary.

To make the filling, place the spinach in a large mixing bowl. Stir in a little less than half the prepared sauce. Season with the black pepper. Set aside. Preheat the oven to 350°.

To make the Sauce Mornay, pour the remaining sauce into the container of an electric blender or food processor. Add the thyme, nutmeg, ¼ cup of the Parmesan, and white or cayenne pepper. Blend until smooth. If the sauce seems too thick, thin it with a little cream or milk.

Spoon about ¼ cup filling in the middle of each crêpe and roll it up; do not tuck in the ends. Arrange the crêpes, seam side down, ½ inch apart, in buttered, oven-to-table baking dishes (if crêpes do not touch, serving is easier). Spread the sauce evenly over the cannelloni. Sprinkle with the remaining ¼ cup grated Parmesan and dot with the tablespoon of butter.

Bake at 350° for 15 to 20 minutes. The top should be lightly browned; if it isn't, slide the dish under a hot broiler for a few seconds. Sprinkle with minced parsley and serve at once.

To Prepare in Advance. Completely assemble the dish but do not bake or add the parsley. Cover with foil and refrigerate up to 48 hours or freeze up to two months. If frozen, thaw overnight, and bake as directed, adding about 10 minutes to the baking time if the dish is still chilled when it is placed in the oven. Sprinkle with parsley; serve at once.

BASIC BEER BATTER CRÊPES
For about 20 five-inch crêpes

    3 large eggs
    1 cup milk
    1 cup beer
    Scant ½ teaspoon salt
    1½ cups Wondra or other instant-blending flour
    3 tablespoons salad oil
    ¼ pound (1 stick) melted butter or margarine

It is best to use an iron French crêpe pan or other pan made especially for crêpes. Season the pan according to manufacturer's directions, and after seasoning, do not wash the pan again. To remove any stubborn spots, scour with kitchen salt and a paper towel.

To make the batter, beat the eggs, then stir in the milk, beer, and salt. Beer adds a delightful flavor and makes very lacy delicate crêpes. Gently stir in the flour; when well-combined add the oil. Refrigerate the batter for at least 6 hours, stirring it from time to time. This allows the flour to be absorbed into the liquid, resulting in a smooth batter and a tender crêpe.

To cook the crêpes, keep your crêpe pan over medium-high heat until a drop of water dances on the surface. With a paper towel or pastry brush, lightly grease the bottom and sides of the pan. With a 2-ounce ladle, pour in a little more than 1 ounce of batter, tipping the pan in a circular motion so that the batter covers the bottom of the pan. The crêpe should be paper thin.

Cook the crêpe on one side for a minute or two until lightly browned—peek underneath by using a spatula; ignore any small holes— then turn it over with the spatula and lightly brown the other side. The first side to brown is the "good" side; the other will look a bit spotty. No matter how expert you become at making crêpes, the first one is never perfect, so use it to test the heat of the pan and the thickness of the batter. If necessary, thin the batter with a little milk.

After the crêpe is cooked on both sides, invert the pan and slide the crêpe onto a clean kitchen towel or piece of foil to cool. As the crêpes are made, stack them neatly, brushing plain melted butter or margarine on each one (the butter will make them easy to separate).

When all the crêpes are cooled and stacked, wrap them in foil, 6 or 8 to a package, and store them in the refrigerator or the freezer.

To Prepare in Advance. Foil-wrapped crêpes can be stored for several days in the refrigerator or for several months in the freezer. When ready to use, be sure they are at room temperature before separating them or they will tear. If you're in a hurry, warm the package in the oven before separating.

QUICHE VON WELANETZ

For 8 generous servings, or 12 medium servings

The Crust

1 recipe Super-Flaky Pastry (recipe follows), or use your favorite pastry recipe for a 9-inch two-crust pie

The Filling

½ pound sliced bacon
1 medium onion, minced
¼ cup freshly grated Parmesan cheese
12 ounces (¾ pound) natural Swiss cheese, grated
7 large eggs
1 teaspoon salt
¼ teaspoon ground nutmeg
⅛ teaspoon cayenne, dissolved in 1 teaspoon water
2 cups light cream (half-and-half)
1 cup heavy cream (whipping cream)

For 32 Servings. Make 3 quiches. If you don't have enough pans, remove the quiche(s) when cool and reuse pans.

Make the pastry and form into a flat patty 6 inches in diameter. Place on a lightly floured pastry cloth or other surface and roll out to form a 14-inch circle. Center the bottom of the spring-form pan on the

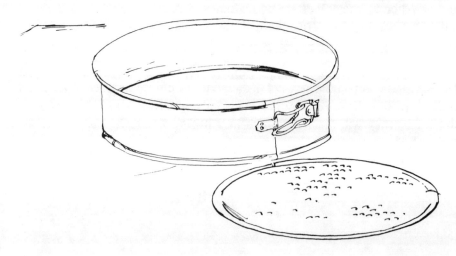

dough and trim the dough 2 inches from the edge all around. Drape the pastry gently around the rolling pin and center it over the pan. Ease it into the pan and with your fingers gently press the pastry into the sides and bottom of the pan. (The pastry shell can be frozen at this point. After it is frozen, remove from the pan and carefully wrap for freezer storage.)

Separate one of the eggs. Place the white in a small dish and the yolk in a large mixing bowl to be used as part of the filling. Beat the white until frothy. Brush the inside surface of the pastry with the white to "waterproof" the pastry. Refrigerate the pastry-lined pan until ready to bake.

Preheat the oven to 375°. Slice the bacon crosswise into ½-inch slices and cook until crisp. Drain on paper towels. Pour out all but 2 teaspoons of bacon fat. In the same skillet, sauté the onions over medium heat about 5 minutes or until they are transparent. Set aside. You are now ready to assemble the quiche.

Sprinkle the grated Parmesan over the bottom of the pastry. Arrange the bacon evenly over cheese and top with the grated Swiss cheese. Place the pan on a square of foil and fold the foil partway up the sides. This will prevent leakage during baking. Now place the pan on a baking sheet for ease in handling.

In a large mixing bowl, beat the eggs with the extra yolk, salt, nutmeg, and diluted cayenne. Beat in the light and heavy creams and sautéed onion only until well combined but not frothy. Slowly pour the liquid over the ingredients in the crust. Bake for 55 to 60 minutes until brown and puffed. The center should feel just firm when pressed with your finger. *Do not overbake or the quiche will be watery.* Cool on a rack for 15 minutes before removing the spring-form sides. The quiche can be served immediately; it is even better cut into slices and reheated as described below.

To Prepare in Advance. Bake up to 24 hours before serving and store *uncovered at room temperature.* Cut into serving slices, place slices about ½ inch apart on baking sheets, and heat at 350° for about 10 minutes. Do not freeze quiche—it will destroy the creamy texture.

SUPER-FLAKY PASTRY IN A FOOD PROCESSOR

Pastry for a 9-inch, 2-crust pie; to line a 9-inch spring-form pan or a 15½-by-10½-by-1-inch jelly roll pan.

1¾ cups Wondra or other instant-blending flour
¾ teaspoon salt
¼ pound (1 stick) butter, chilled (do not use margarine)
¼ cup Crisco, chilled
¼ cup *ice* water (see *Note*)
Optional additions when you need a sweet crust: ¼ cup sugar and
   1 teaspoon minced lemon zest (yellow peel)
All-purpose flour for rolling out the dough

Note: Reduce water on hot, humid days; add a bit more on dry days.

Place the flour and salt in the container of a food processor equipped with a steel blade. Cut the butter into 8 crosswise slices, then cut in half lengthwise. Transfer the 16 bits to the food processor and blend, turning the motor on and off for about 4 seconds, until the butter is the size of corn kernels. Remove the lid and add the Crisco in about 6 pieces, distributing evenly around the blade. Replace the lid; while processing pour the cold water in an even stream through the feed tube. When half the water has been added, stop the motor and scrape down the sides of the container with a rubber spatula. Add the remaining water, and blend just until the dough begins to form one mass that follows the blade. The dough will feel soft and pliable at this point.

Using a rubber spatula, transfer the dough to a piece of plastic wrap which has been generously sprinkled with all-purpose flour. Depending on the shape you want, form the dough into a rectangular or round patty, wrap tightly, and refrigerate for 30 minutes to relax the gluten and make rolling easier.

(We always use a pastry cloth, generously sprinkled with flour, when rolling out pastry. The cloth makes cleanup a breeze.)

To Prepare in Advance. Store the dough in the refrigerator up to four days or freeze. If frozen, thaw in the refrigerator overnight. If the dough is too firm to roll out, soften at room temperature for 15 to 30 minutes.

MINTED FRUIT CUPS

½ fresh pineapple, cut in chunks
2 cups melon cubes or balls (watermelon, honeydew, or melon of
   your choice)

2 oranges, peeled, cleaned of all white membrane, diced, and
  seeded
1 tablespoon orange liqueur or brandy

The Garnish

8 tiny sprigs fresh mint (can substitute parsley, small daisies, or
  other nontoxic flowers)

In a mixing bowl combine the pineapple, melon, and orange
pieces. Sprinkle with orange liqueur or brandy and marinate in the
refrigerator for at least 2 hours. Arrange the salad in serving dishes (we
use 3- to 4-ounce-capacity miniature soufflé dishes) on a tray large
enough to hold them snugly. Garnish each serving with a sprig of mint,
parsley, or a flower.

To Prepare in Advance. The salad can be placed in the serving dishes up
to 8 hours before serving. Cover with a damp towel and place in the
refrigerator until ready to serve.

HERBED PITA ROUNDS

8 rounds plain or sesame pita bread (to make 16 halves)
¼ pound (1 stick) butter or margarine, at room temperature
Herb seasoning of your choice, to taste (see *Note*)

Note: Use your favorite herb seasoning or experiment with different
combinations. We like the Villa de Vero brand, available at specialty
food stores. Or, try a combination of ¼ teaspoon dried thyme, ⅛
teaspoon poultry seasoning, and ⅛ teaspoon paprika.

Preheat oven to 350°. Split each pita into two rounds. The easiest way to do this is to cut around ⅛-inch from the edge with kitchen scissors. Spread each circle with butter or margarine and sprinkle lightly with herbs. Arrange the rounds on a baking sheet and toast at 350° for 7 to 10 minutes or until crisp and golden. Serve hot on a warm plate or in a basket.

To Prepare in Advance. The pita can be prepared and toasted up to 8 hours ahead. Cool, then store in a plastic bag at room temperature. Reheat on a baking sheet in a 350° oven and serve piping hot.

ICED STRAWBERRY SOUFFLÉ

6 cups fresh strawberries, or 1½ pounds frozen unsweetened strawberries, thawed
2 tablespoons (2 envelopes) unflavored gelatin
¾ cup sugar
½ cup cold water
3 egg whites
2 teaspoons fresh lemon juice
1½ cups heavy cream (whipping cream)

The Garnish

⅓ cup heavy cream, whipped and sweetened to taste
8 strawberries, plain or chocolate dipped (recipe follows)
8 sprigs mint

For 16 Servings. Double the recipe. Serve in two 6-cup soufflé dishes, one 12-cup soufflé dish, or 16 individual soufflé dishes.

Collar the soufflé dish(es) with oiled wax paper or aluminum foil. Cut the paper long enough to go around the soufflé dish(es) with a generous overlap. Fold the paper in halves or thirds lengthwise and tie with a string to form a collar 2 inches higher than the rim of the dish.

Wash the fresh strawberries quickly under cold running water. Hull and dry them on paper towels. Purée the berries, about 2 cups at a time, in a blender or food processor fitted with the steel blade. Pour the purée into a large mixing bowl.

In a small heavy saucepan, combine the gelatin, ½ cup of the sugar, and the cold water. Stir over very low heat just until the gelatin and sugar are dissolved. Cool to room temperature. Stir the gelatin mixture into the puréed strawberries. Chill until the mixture mounds slightly when dropped from a spoon. (To speed the setting process, set the bowl in a larger bowl partly filled with ice. Chill at room temperature, stirring often, until thickened.)

Beat the egg whites with the lemon juice until soft peaks form when beater is lifted. Gradually add the remaining ¼ cup sugar, beating until the meringue stands in firm peaks. Using a rubber spatula, gently transfer the egg whites on top of the strawberry mixture. Set aside. Use the same mixing bowl to whip the cream until stiff. Fold the meringue into the strawberry mixture, then fold in the whipped cream. No streaks of white should remain, but do not overmix. Pour into the prepared dish(es). Chill large soufflés at least 4 hours, small soufflés at least 2 hours.

Carefully remove collar before serving. To decorate, spoon small dollops of sweetened whipped cream around the rim of the large soufflé or in the center of each small soufflé. Top each with a plain or chocolate-dipped strawberry and add a sprig of mint.

To Prepare in Advance. The soufflé(s) will keep for 2 days in the refrigerator or for several weeks in the freezer. If frozen, thaw overnight in the refrigerator before serving.

CHOCOLATE-DIPPED STRAWBERRIES
    6 ounces dark dipping chocolate (see *Note 1*)
    1½ teaspoons vegetable oil
    24 large perfect strawberries with stems (see *Note 2*)

Note 1: We use a dipping chocolate called Parker, made by the Nestlé Company. Baker's German's Sweet Chocolate may also be used, but the result will not be as shiny and dazzling as the dipping chocolate. If you use Baker's, omit the oil.

Note 2: It is easier to put "stems" on strawberries than to pay the exorbitant price asked for stemmed ones. Use a skewer to poke a hole in the stem end. Dip a 3-inch piece of parsley stem in melted chocolate and insert it in the hole. Chill until firm. The chocolate will harden and secure it in place.

Rinse and thoroughly dry the strawberries on paper towels. Chop the chocolate coarsely into the top of a double boiler, and place over hot, not boiling, water, stirring just until dissolved. Remove from heat and stir in the oil. Insert a sturdy toothpick into the base of each strawberry, next to the stem. Holding onto the toothpick, dip each strawberry into the chocolate, coating it three-quarters of the way to the top. Leave the green hull and some red visible for a more decorative effect. Spear the free end of the toothpick into a piece of Styrofoam or a grapefruit so that the strawberry can dry upside down. Or after dipping let the strawberries harden on wax paper. Chill until serving time.

Serve the strawberries as they are by removing the toothpicks and serving 3 on a small plate per person, or prepare 1 strawberry per person when used as a garnish to top the Iced Strawberry Soufflé.

To Prepare in Advance. We have successfully kept dipped strawberries up to 36 hours. However, the shorter the time the better. Keep chilled, but do not freeze.

Afterthought. For still another taste delight, with a cook's hypodermic needle, inject a few cc's of Grand Marnier in the center of each berry. The needle can be purchased in cookstores or your doctor might provide you with one if you tell him why you want it.

ENCORES

The White Sangría will lose its sparkle and be diluted from the ice, but if a considerable amount remains, restore it by adding some orange liqueur and any leftover fruit salad for flavor and fresh champagne or club soda for sparkle. Leftover mangoes can be used to make the Mango Sherbert in the Mexican Fiesta Buffet.

You will have heated only the required number of quiche slices for the buffet, so any leftovers can be served that same evening. Or you can refrigerate the slices for another time, although they will suffer slightly in texture. Refrigerate any unserved cannelloni. It will still be delicious but a bit tired looking. To serve, freshen the top with a sprinkling of Parmesan and heat gently just until hot. Sprinkle with a small amount of minced parsley. The pita rounds also reheat very nicely.

Freeze any remaining individual soufflés for another occasion. If the soufflé was served from a large dish, spoon portions into champagne glasses, top with Chocolate-Dipped Strawberries, and serve within 24 hours.

EXOTIC BUFFET

CURRY

CHUTNEY

Menu

Champagne, Red and White Wines

or

Framboise Punch with Fern Ice Ring *(Summer)*

or

Champagne–Cassis Punch *(Winter)*

Boursin-Stuffed Mushrooms

Crab, Chicken or Turkey Curry

Rice

Full-bodied White Wine

Chutneys
Fresh Mint Chutney Taj Mahal
Fresh Nectarine Chutney
Cranberry Chutney
Fresh Cherry or Purple Plum Chutney

Condiments
Fresh Pineapple
Watermelon Rind Pickles
Sliced Cucumbers
Scallions
Toasted Coconut
Dried Currants
Unsalted Peanuts

Assorted Finger-Food Sweets
Miniature Strawberry Tarts
Sunshine Squares
Black Bottom Cups
Creamy Caramels with Walnuts
Macademia Nut Candy Mauna Kea

Coffee and Tea

EXOTIC CURRY AND
CHUTNEY BUFFET

For years we wanted to create a perfect buffet dish, suitable for any size group that could be made far in advance, served day or night, would be easy to eat, and appeal to the broadest range of tastes. This is it!

Since we have four chutneys and seven condiments, guests can go all-out in exploring these colorful and taste-tempting accompaniments. To serve the condiments we use a seven-section, flower-shaped lucite serving dish. Refills are kept in the kitchen so that the dishes can be quickly and easily replenished as the supply diminishes.

The inevitable rice is here but the recipe is perfect. You cook it ahead, so there is no last-minute panic. Rice kernels stay beautifully dry and separate.

The spicy and aromatic Fresh Mint Chutney Taj Mahal is a great chutney for which no cooking is required (it takes just seconds to make in a blender). We are grateful to Debbie Chaddah, co-owner of the Taj Mahal Restaurant in Minneapolis for sharing her specialty with us, and to Cecily Brownstone for sharing the freshest-tasting chutney we've ever had, one made with nectarines.

Among the suggested punches is one we concocted—the gloriously beautiful Framboise Punch. Framboise is a colorless brandy made from raspberries; when combined with fresh raspberries and champagne it becomes the ultimate in party drinks.

If this is a large party and you have arranged to serve champagne, it may be served throughout the meal. Ideally, this curry should be served with a full-bodied white wine, such as a chilled Pouilly-Fumé, which can stand up to such a spicy dish. But have a bottle or two of red wine on hand for the few who may insist on it.

57

As for those desserts—the miniature Strawberry Tarts are perfect for a large tea, buffet, or cocktail party. The filling and the glaze were adapted from a Thermador microwave oven recipe for Frech Strawberry Pie; we transformed the pie into small tarts and topped each with a single glazed strawberry. The Sunshine Squares are Betty Lou Port's happy variation of the now classic Lemon Squares—a trinity of textures: rich crust, tangy filling, powdery topping. Harriet Antelyes claims the Black Bottom Cups' recipe has been around for years. They are new to us—and we think they need a revival. They are delightful to set out as part of an assortment at large parties. Creamy Caramels with Walnuts are worth every minute of the candy thermometer watching they demand.

One of the highlights of our 1978 "Culinary Entertaining" seminar was our stay at the Mauna Kea Beach Hotel on the island of Hawaii. Among the many who made us feel welcome was head chef, Achim (Kim) Dietrich, who shared his macadamia nut candy recipe with us—proving in more ways than one that travel is "broadening." As an alternate to the pastel coating used by the hotel, we have improvised with many meltable coatings—milk chocolate, white chocolate, and others—all are wonderful.

The recipe for Boursin-Stuffed Mushrooms appears in the Elegant Open House Buffet.

THE TABLE SETTINGS

This is an any-occasion or time-of-day, single-line buffet that requires fork only. Wine, appetizer, desserts, and beverages are served separately.

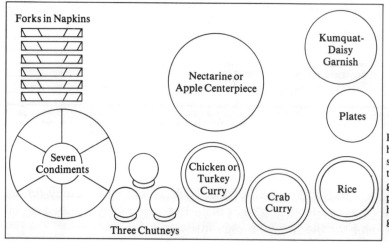

Step 1   Step 2

Centerpieces

Buffet and Dining Tables. For summer, make Lemon or Nectarine Trees; for winter, Apple or Pear Trees. For each centerpiece, besides the fruit, you will need 3 plates (dinner, salad, and saucer size), doilies to fit the plates, and 2 champagne glasses. Arrange the centerpiece on a footed cake stand for the buffet table, on plates for the dining tables. Cut a thin slice from the end of each fruit so that it will stand without rolling. Cover each dish with a matching doily. Now tier the plates, using the champagne glasses. Place a close ring of fruit around the rims of the two bottom plates. In the saucer, place 3 pieces of fruit, top with a single fruit. Spray with nonstick cooking spray to give the fruit a sheen. Insert clusters of parsley set in water tubes in the spaces between the fruits. In summer, stud the parsley with small white daisies or bunches of baby's breath; in winter, use walnuts and cinnamon sticks. The trees can be prepared the day before; add parsley and flowers 1 hour before guests arrive.

TIMETABLE

The time of day or evening you serve your buffet will influence your preparation schedule. No appetizer is necessary at a luncheon, but dinner guests expect something to nibble on with the champagne or punch, even if the occasion is an open house and the buffet table is used. If champagne is to be served, arrange for tubs in which the bottles can be iced.

Very few items in this menu need last-minute preparation. The basic curry sauce freezes well, as do all the chutneys, or they can be made a week in advance and refrigerated. Most of the desserts can be made days or even weeks ahead, including the pastry shells for the miniature tarts, which can be frozen.

The Day Before the Party. Prepare handwritten place cards to identify the curries and chutneys and set them in place. Cook the rice and refrigerate. Prepare the pineapple and scallion condiments. Stock up on tubs to hold the ice cubes and champagne, or, if you are serving a punch, make an ice ring (see Ice Rings in Garnishes appendix).

On the Day of the Party. In the morning, stuff the mushrooms, sprinkling with parsley if serving them cold, or with paprika if they are to be broiled. Refrigerate. Prepare the rest of the condiments. Assemble and garnish the tarts and arrange them on a doily-covered dish ready for serving. Chill until serving time. Assemble an assortment of the other sweets on one or more trays, cover with plastic wrap, and leave at room temperature. Prepare the Kumquat-Daisy garnishes.

COUNTDOWN

1 hour before guests arrive:	Set out all the chutneys and condiments on the buffet table.
30 minutes before guests arrive:	Chill the champagne.
	Place curry sauce in two large pots or heat slowly in crock-pots with removable crockery liners.
	Set out mushrooms and garnish with parsley.
	Bring rice to room temperature.
15 minutes before guests arrive:	Unmold the ice ring and place in the punch bowl.
	Rinse and drain raspberries for punch.
	Prepare coffee and tea.
As guests arrive:	Combine punch ingredients in punch bowl.
30 minutes before serving:	Heat rice in a 350° oven for 20 minutes. Fill serving dishes with hot water to warm them. Dry before using. When hot, transfer rice to warmed serving dish.
	Heat water for chafing dish water-bath, if using chafing dishes.

5 minutes before serving:

Heat the curry sauce, if not already hot, and add cooked crab to one portion, cooked chicken or turkey to the other.

Pour hot water in chafing dish bottom (water-bath), then ladle in hot curries.

Announce the serving.

Set out the dessert trays when the main course is served. They require no further attention.

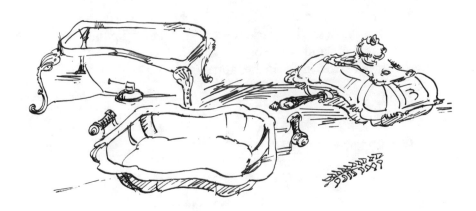

RECIPES

FRAMBOISE PUNCH
For 24 servings

 6 fifths or 3 magnums champagne, chilled
 1½ cups Framboise (raspberry *eau de vie*), chilled
 2 baskets fresh raspberries, washed
 Syrup to taste (see *Note*)

To Serve

Fern Ice Ring (see Ice Rings in Garnishes appendix)

Note. Framboise is "dry," and if your champagne is "brut" (the driest type), you may wish to sweeten the mixture. Use a simple sugar syrup: equal parts sugar and water boiled together in a small pan until the sugar is dissolved. Add about 2 tablespoons of syrup for each fifth of champagne.

Just before serving, combine the champagne and Framboise in a punch bowl. Add the raspberries and ice ring. Sweeten to taste with the syrup.

Afterthought. Though not appropriate for this menu because strawberries are used in the dessert, a variation of this beautiful punch is to use a strawberry liqueur and strawberries speared with mint (see Long-Stemmed Strawberries in Garnishes appendix).

CHAMPAGNE-CASSIS PUNCH
For 24 servings

¾ cup (6 ounces) Créme de Cassis (black currant liqueur)
⅓ cup freshly squeezed, strained lemon juice
6 fifths or 3 magnums champagne, chilled

To Serve

Lemon Ice Ring or Mint Ice Ring (see Ice Rings in Garnishes appendix)
½ to 1 lemon, thinly sliced

Just before serving, unmold the ice ring into a punch bowl and pour in the Créme de Cassis and lemon juice. Add the chilled champagne. Float lemon slices on surface and serve immediately.

To Prepare in Advance. Combine Créme de Cassis and lemon juice in a pitcher, cover, and store in the refrigerator. Just before serving, pour into a punch bowl and add champagne, ice ring, and lemon slices.

CRAB, CHICKEN OR TURKEY CURRY
For 24 servings

¾ pound (3 sticks) butter or margarine
4 cups finely diced onions
4 cups finely diced, peeled tart green apples (such as Pippins)
5 cloves garlic, pressed
½ to ¾ cup imported Madras curry powder (preferably Sun Brand
  label), the amount depending on how hot you like curry
4 teaspoons celery salt
1 teaspoon dried thyme leaves, crumbled
2 cups rich chicken broth (undiluted, if canned)
1 cup dry French vermouth, or 1¼ cups dry white wine
½ cup pale dry sherry
3 cups heavy cream (whipping cream)
2 cups light cream (half-and-half)
½ cup puréed mango chutney (optional)
2 tablespoons cornstarch, dissolved in ¼ cup cold water

For crab curry: 1 pound crabmeat, shredded, and picked over (see *Note*)

For chicken or turkey curry: 1 pound cooked chicken or turkey,
shredded (see *Note*)

To Serve
Rice (recipe follows)
4 chutneys (recipes follow)
7 condiments (directions follow): 1 fresh pineapple, 2 (19-ounce)
  jars of watermelon rind pickles, 2 medium cucumbers, 2 bunches
  scallions, 2 cups flaked, toasted, coconut, ¾ pound dried currants, 1 (8-ounce) jar unsalted peanuts.

The Garnish (for each plate)
½ preserved kumquat, halved lengthwise, laid flat, and speared
  with a single daisy (an 8-ounce bottle of kumquats should be
  adequate)

Note: If serving only *one* curry, use two pounds of crabmeat *or* two
pounds of chicken or turkey.

Melt the butter in a heavy pot of at least 6-quart capacity. Sauté the onions, apples, and garlic for 5 minutes or until the onion is transparent. Stir in the curry powder, celery salt, and thyme, and cook over medium-low heat,
(longer won't hurt) to eliminate the raw taste of the curry powder. Add the broth, vermouth or wine, and sherry. Bring the mixture to a boil, lower heat, and simmer slowly for 15 minutes. Stir in the cream, half-and-half, and chutney, and bring to a simmer. Taste and add salt if needed. To thicken the sauce, slowly pour in the cornstarch and water mixture and stir until thickened, 1 or 2 minutes.

Just before serving, divide the sauce in two parts. Add the crab-meat to one and the chicken or turkey to the other and simmer long enough to heat through. Transfer to large chafing dishes or crock-pots with removable crockery servers. Serve hot with rice, chutneys, and condiments.

To Prepare in Advance. The basic curry sauce can be refrigerated up to four days. Do not add the meat until you heat the sauce. If the sauce is frozen, it will need to be rethickened with cornstarch, following the same directions given in the recipe, because cornstarch breaks down and loses its thickening power when frozen. If making this sauce specifically for freezer storage, omit the thickening step until after you have thawed the sauce and are heating it to serve. Add the cornstarch as described above. When the sauce is thickened, add the meat and heat through.

RICE
For 24 servings

  6 cups long-grain rice
  2 tablespoons salt

Bring 6 quarts of water to a rapid boil in a 10- to 12-quart pot. Gradually sprinkle in the rice. Simmer uncovered, without stirring, for 12 to 18 minutes. Test for doneness after 12 minutes. When the rice is tender, transfer to colander and rinse with cold water. With the end of a wooden spoon, poke a few holes in the rice to help the rice cool. Let it drain thoroughly up to 30 minutes. Transfer the cooked rice to a buttered baking dish, layering it no deeper than 2 inches. Cover loosely with foil and refrigerate.

Before serving, reheat the rice, still covered with foil, in a 350° oven for about 20 minutes until very hot. Fluff with a fork and place in a heated serving dish.

To Prepare in Advance. Cook the rice up to two days before serving and refrigerate. Follow reheating directions above.

FRESH MINT CHUTNEY TAJ MAHAL
For 2 cups

20 large sprigs of fresh mint (approximately 100 mint leaves)
2 medium onions, coarsely chopped
8 hot green chile peppers, preferably jalapenos (see *Note*)
¼ cup freshly squeezed, strained lemon juice
¼ cup cold water
4 teaspoons coriander seeds
2 teaspoons salt

Note: We use canned jalapeños, rinsed and seeded, though fresh can also be used. This chutney is decidedly "hot"; caution guests to use sparingly or use fewer chiles if you prefer a milder flavor.

Wash and dry the mint well. Pick off the leaves and discard the stalks. Place the leaves in an electric blender with all the remaining ingredients. Blend at low speed until the mixture is running smoothly through the blades. Stop the motor once or twice to scrape down the sides of the container with a rubber spatula. Blend at high speed for 3 or 4 minutes or until the chutney is smooth. Cool. Transfer to plastic or glass containers and refrigerate for 24 hours to allow flavors to ripen before serving.

To Prepare in Advance. The chutney can be stored up to one week in the refrigerator and frozen up to three months.

FRESH NECTARINE CHUTNEY

1 cup firmly packed light brown sugar
½ cup cider vinegar
4 or 5 unpeeled nectarines, pitted and diced to measure 2½ to 3 cups
1 cup golden or dark raisins (or ½ cup each variety)
½ lemon, unpeeled, very thinly sliced
2 tablespoons finely chopped ginger root (see *Note*)
1 clove garlic, minced
½ teaspoon salt
⅛ teaspoon cayenne

Note: You can substitute 2½ tablespoons of chopped crystallized ginger. Rinse it in hot water to soften slightly.

In a large enamel or stainless-steel saucepan, bring the sugar and vinegar to a boil, stirring constantly until the sugar dissolves. Add the remaining ingredients. Reduce heat and bring mixture to a simmer. Remove from heat; cover and let stand until cool. Transfer the chutney into a 1-quart refrigerator container. Cover it tightly and store in the refrigerator. Bring to room temperature before serving.

To Prepare in Advance. Store in the refrigerator up to two weeks or in the freezer up to four months. Bring to room temperature before serving.

CRANBERRY CHUTNEY

For 4 cups, or up to 32 servings

4 cups (about 1 pound) fresh cranberries
2 cups water
1 cup sugar
½ cup cider vinegar
1 medium onion, finely chopped
1 large clove garlic, minced
1 tablespoon ground cinnamon
¼ teaspoon ground allspice
1 teaspoon salt
⅛ teaspoon cayenne
1 cup seedless raisins or chopped pitted dates
1 cup dried currants

⅔ cup firmly packed dark brown sugar
½ cup finely diced crystallized ginger
1 cup slivered blanched almonds or other nuts

Note: For year-round use, buy cranberries in season and store them in the freezer right in the bag in which you bought them.

Rinse the cranberries and pick them over, discarding the soft ones. Set aside.

Combine the water, sugar, vinegar, onion, garlic, cinnamon, allspice, salt, and cayenne in a 4-quart enamel or stainless-steel saucepan. Bring to a boil, lower the heat, and simmer uncovered for 5 minutes. Stir in the cranberries and the remaining ingredients, except the nuts; simmer 10 minutes longer. Stir in the nuts, cool, and refrigerate. Serve at room temperature.

To Prepare in Advance. The flavor is enhanced if the chutney is made at least 24 hours before serving. It will keep a year or more in the refrigerator or freezer.

FRESH CHERRY OR PURPLE PLUM CHUTNEY
For 5 cups

6 cups (3 pounds) fresh Bing cherries or purple plums, pitted (see *Note 1*)
3 cups cider vinegar
1½ cups sugar
1½ cups seedless raisins
2 medium onions, minced
½ cup (4 ounces) minced candied ginger (see *Note 2*)
2 tablespoons yellow mustard seeds
2 teaspoons ground cinnamon
1½ teaspoons salt
½ teaspoon ground allspice
½ teaspoon ground cloves
¼ teaspoon ground mace or freshly grated nutmeg

Note 1: Cherry pitters are available at cookware shops and hardware stores.

Note 2: Candied ginger is usually cheaper when purchased in plastic boxes (available during the holidays or in Oriental markets) than in spice bottles.

Combine all the ingredients in a heavy-bottomed stainless-steel or enamel saucepan of at least 6-quart capacity. Bring to a boil, then lower the heat. Simmer, covered, 1 hour. Remove the lid and simmer, uncovered, about 40 minutes longer or until thick. Stir the chutney frequently toward the end of the cooking time to prevent sticking; reduce the heat if necessary. Cool. Transfer the chutney to plastic containers with lids for refrigerator or freezer storage. For best flavor, serve at room temperature.

To Prepare in Advance. The chutney will keep just about forever in the refrigerator. It also freezes perfectly.

SEVEN CONDIMENTS

Fresh Pineapple. Remove the rind from a large fresh pineapple and cut the pineapple lengthwise into eighths, remove core, then cut crosswise into thin wedge-shaped slivers. Refrigerate, covered, up to 24 hours.

Watermelon Rind Pickles. Pickled watermelon rind is too exotic for some people, but it is a wonderful condiment. Drain two 19-ounce jars of commercial watermelon rind pickles. Serve with a pickle fork.

Sliced Cucumbers. Peel 2 medium cucumbers and slice them in half lengthwise. Scoop out and discard the seeds with the tip of a spoon. Cut the halves into thin slices. (Cucumber seeds can cause indigestion unless you use cellophane-wrapped "hothouse" cucumbers.)

Scallions. Cut two bunches of scallions (about 12) into thin slices, including some of the green tops. Cover with a damp paper towel and refrigerate up to 24 hours.

Toasted Coconut. Spread about 1 pound unsweetened flaked coconut on a large baking sheet. Bake in the center of a 350° oven about 10 minutes, stirring occasionally, until lightly browned. Cool, then store in a sealed plastic bag in the freezer up to several months.

Dried Currants. A ¾ pound box will yield about 2 cups currants. You can substitute raisins but we prefer currants, which are daintier.

Unsalted Peanuts. If you prefer, use about 1 pound shelled, unsalted roasted peanuts instead of an 8-ounce jar.

MINIATURE STRAWBERRY TARTS
For 32 tarts

> 32 Miniature Tart Shells (recipe follows)
> 4 boxes (about 12 cups) fresh strawberries, washed, dried, and hulled
> 3 tablespoons cornstarch
> 1¼ cups sugar
> 1½ teaspoons Grand Marnier
> 1½ teaspoons freshly squeezed lemon juice
> Red food coloring

The Cream Cheese Filling

> 6 ounces cream cheese
> ½ cup sugar
> ½ cup heavy cream (whipping cream), whipped
> ½ teaspoon vanilla extract

The Garnish

> 32 small mint leaves

Purée 3 cups (about 1 box) of the least perfect strawberries in a blender or food processor. Add sufficient water, if needed, to measure 1½ cups purée. Reserve the perfect strawberries for the tops of the tarts.

In a heavy-bottomed saucepan (for stovetop cooking) or an 8-cup glass measure (for microwave cooking), stir the cornstarch and sugar together until evenly blended. Stir in the strawberry purée and cook for 5 to 6 minutes, stirring constantly on medium heat on top of the stove or stirring every minute or so on "high" in a microwave oven. The mixture should come to a rolling boil and thicken. Stir in the Grand Marnier, lemon juice, and a few drops of red coloring to make a bright, ruby-red glaze. Cool until lukewarm.

Meanwhile, make the cream cheese filling. Soften the cream cheese by melting it slightly in the top of a double boiler placed over hot water or by placing it in a glass measure in a microwave oven for 15 seconds on "high." Blend in the sugar and vanilla extract. Fold in the whipped cream.

To assemble the tarts, place about a teaspoonful of the cream cheese mixture in the bottom of each tart shell. Press in a perfect strawberry, hull side down. Spoon in just enough lukewarm glaze to cover the strawberry and the cream cheese filling. Do not let the glaze flow over the rim of the shell. Chill. Garnish each tart with a small mint leaf before serving.

To Prepare in Advance. The pastry shells freeze well. It is best to make the filling and glaze the day of the party. Fill the tarts within 6 hours of serving and keep chilled.

Afterthought. The same filling, strawberries, and glaze can be used to fill a deep 9-inch pie shell.

MINIATURE TART SHELLS
For 40 to 50 shells

> 1 recipe Super-Flaky Pastry (see Recipes index), with ¼ cup sugar and 1 teaspoon lemon zest (yellow peel) added to the flour during the mixing, or use your favorite recipe for two, 9-inch pie crusts with the added ingredients

You will need at least two miniature muffin tins, with the cups measuring 1¾ x ¾ inch.

Preheat the oven to 400°. Roll out half the pastry and cut into 2½-to 2¾-inch rounds, using a plain or scalloped cutter or the top of a drinking glass. Center the rounds on the *back* of the tin over each muffin cup. Cover with another muffin tin, pressing down gently (take care not to tear the dough) to mold the dough over each cup. (For best results chill the dough in the freezer for 10 minutes before baking; this will prevent shrinkage.)

Keep the shells between the two tins and bake in the center of the oven for 10 minutes. Remove the upper pan, prick the bottom of each shell in two or three places with the tines of a fork; return the shells uncovered to the oven to brown for 5 to 8 minutes. Watch carefully so they do not burn. Cool briefly, then gently turn the shells onto a towel to cool.

Repeat with the remaining dough. When you remove the top tin, you can place circles of dough on the back of it while waiting for the other pan to be free. When we make these we use four pans, so we have two batches going at the same time.

To Prepare in Advance. The shells can be stored in a plastic bag at room temperature up to three days or frozen up to two months. Refrigeration is not recommended—it toughens the shells.

SUNSHINE SQUARES
For 24 squares

The Crust
¼ pound (1 stick) butter or margarine, at room temperature
½ cup powdered sugar
2 cups sifted all-purpose flour
Dash salt

The Topping
4 large eggs
2 cups granulated sugar
¼ cup all-purpose flour
¼ cup freshly squeezed, strained lemon juice
¼ cup freshly squeezed, strained orange juice
1½ teaspoons lemon zest (yellow peel), finely chopped
1½ teaspoons orange zest (orange peel), finely chopped
About ¾ cup powdered sugar

Preheat the oven to 350°. Spray a shallow 9 x 13-inch baking dish lightly with nonstick cooking spray or line it with foil.

Mix the crust ingredients with a fork or electric mixer until well combined. Pat into the bottom of the baking pan. Bake for 20 minutes. Remove the pan from the oven and let the crust cool.

Meanwhile, prepare the topping. In a large mixing bowl, beat the eggs and sugar together until very creamy. Add the flour, citrus juices, and zests. Beat to combine thoroughly and pour the mixture over the crust. Return to the oven and bake about 20 minutes or until the topping has set. It should be firm when pressed with your fingertip. Cool. Sprinkle a heavy even layer of powdered sugar over the top by pressing the sugar through a strainer with the back of a spoon. Cut into 24 squares and remove from pan.

To Prepare in Advance. The squares can be wrapped in foil and stored up to four days at room temperature. They freeze well up to six months. Sprinkle with more powdered sugar to freshen their appearance before serving.

BLACK BOTTOM CUPS
For 48 miniature cupcakes

The Filling
1 (8-ounce) package cream cheese
1 egg
⅓ cup sugar
⅛ teaspoon salt
1 (6-ounce) package semi-sweet chocolate morsels

The Cake Batter
1½ cups sifted all-purpose flour
1 cup sugar
1 cup water
⅓ cup vegetable oil
¼ cup unsweetened cocoa powder
1 tablespoon white vinegar
1 teaspoon vanilla extract

You will need four miniature muffin tins, the same as used for the Miniature Strawberry Tarts. For easy removal, spray the inside of the muffin tins with nonstick cooking spray. Preheat the oven to 350°.

To make the filling, in a small mixing bowl beat the cream cheese until fluffy. Beat in the egg, sugar, and salt until well combined. Fold in the chocolate morsels. Set aside.

To make the cake batter, beat all the ingredients together until very well blended. Fill the muffin cups two-thirds full of batter. Place about 1 teaspoon of the cream cheese mixture in the center of the batter. This will sink into the cupcake to make a filling. Bake the cupcakes in the lower third of the oven for 12 to 15 minutes. The filling should not brown. Cool on a rack for 15 minutes, then turn the cupcakes out of the tins to finish cooling on racks.

To Prepare in Advance. These cupcakes can be stored in plastic wrap or in foil pie tins inside a plastic bag at room temperature up to two days. They freeze beautifully if made up to two months ahead. (We have found that refrigerating baked goods tends to dry them, so we prefer room temperature storage or freezing.)

CREAMY CARAMELS WITH WALNUTS
For 60 squares

> 2 cups sugar
> 1 cup light corn syrup (Karo)
> 3 cups heavy cream (whipping cream)
> 60 perfect walnut halves (see *Note*)

Note: Perfect walnut halves can be purchased at shops that specialize in nuts. If you wish to shell them yourself, stand the nuts on end and tap lightly with a hammer. They should split into two perfect halves. Remove from their shells. If they break imperfectly, you can eat your mistakes!

In a heavy-bottomed saucepan of at least 4-quart capacity, combine the sugar, corn syrup, and 1 cup of the cream. Bring to a boil while stirring, then lower the heat and simmer slowly (about 30 minutes) to the soft-ball stage (238° on a candy thermometer).

It is best to use an accurate candy thermometer for making candy, although a cold water test works just as well. When you think the candy is almost done, drop no more than ½ teaspoon of the hot syrup from a spoon into cold—not ice—water. Let it stand in the water for 1 minute, then pick up the candy with your fingers. "Soft-ball" stage means that the syrup makes a soft ball when you pick it up, but it does not hold its shape. "Firm-ball" stage means it makes a firm ball that holds its shape when picked up.)

Stir in 1 more cup of cream and simmer about another 30 minutes to the "medium-ball" stage (242°). Stir in the remaining cup of cream and simmer, stirring often, about another 30 minutes to the "firm-ball" stage (246°). Pour the mixture into a lightly buttered shallow dish. Press the walnut halves over the top close together in even rows. Cool about 4 hours until firm. Turn out of the pan and place, right side up, on a cutting board. Use a heavy, sharp knife dipped in hot water to cut the caramels into squares. Wrap individually in plastic wrap.

To Prepare in Advance. If stored in a cool place in an airtight container (such as a candy tin), the caramels will keep at least one month. They can be frozen up to six months in advance.

MACADAMIA NUT CANDY MAUNA KEA
For about 20 pieces

> 8 ounces pastel or chocolate candy coating, or milk chocolate (see *Note*)
> 4 ounces macadamia nuts (or other nuts of your choice)

Note: Chef Kim Dietrich of the Mauna Kea Beach Hotel uses Nestle's "Icecap" coating, which we found at the Farmer's Market in Los Angeles at a candy-making booth. The coating comes in coarsely broken chunks. Candy coatings of this type are preferable to regular milk chocolate because they do not melt easily in storage. Milk chocolate-coated nuts should be stored in the refrigerator.

To melt the coating, cut in small pieces into the top of a double boiler and place over hot water. Stir just until melted and remove from heat.

Meanwhile, shake the macadamia nuts in a strainer to remove the powdery grains of salt. Rub the nuts in a towel to remove as much of the remaining salt as possible. Stir the nuts into the melted coating. With a spoon lift 3 coated nuts at a time and form a cluster on wax paper. Set aside to cool. Then place each cluster in a frilled candy cup (available at gourmet supply shops), ready to serve.

To Prepare in Advance. This confection will keep for weeks if packed in an airtight tin and set in a cool place—they will last, that is, if you can resist them that long.

ENCORES

Treat your friends and neighbors to the fresh tarts and the punch. Everything else is just as great the second time around as it was the first. Refrigerate perishables and store the candies in airtight tins. Then within the next few days polish off the other leftovers.

The fruit from the centerpieces can be recycled. If you used nectarines, make more Fresh Nectarine Chutney to store in the freezer for your next curry party. The apples can be eaten fresh or made into an open-face French tart by substituting apples for the pears in the Pear Tart (recipe appears in our Olde English Roast Beef Buffet).

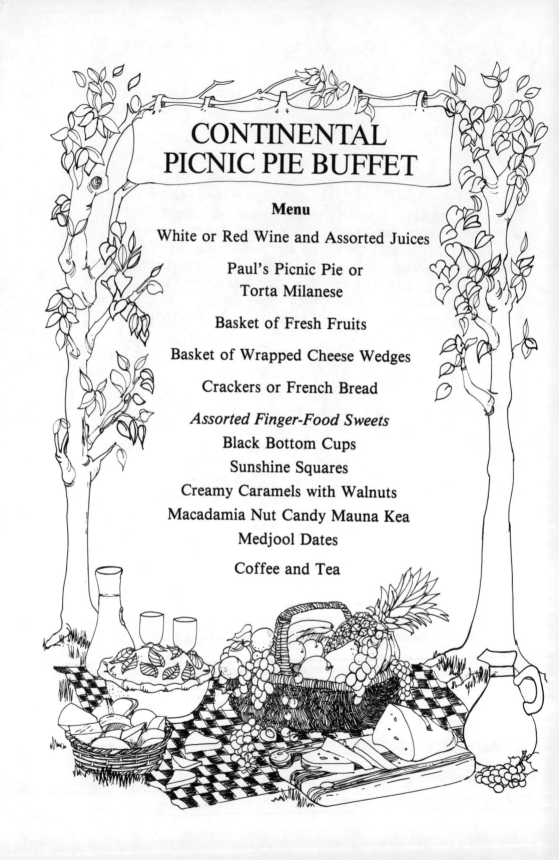

CONTINENTAL PICNIC PIE BUFFET

Menu

White or Red Wine and Assorted Juices

Paul's Picnic Pie or
Torta Milanese

Basket of Fresh Fruits

Basket of Wrapped Cheese Wedges

Crackers or French Bread

Assorted Finger-Food Sweets
Black Bottom Cups
Sunshine Squares
Creamy Caramels with Walnuts
Macadamia Nut Candy Mauna Kea
Medjool Dates

Coffee and Tea

CONTINENTAL AL FRESCO
PICNIC PIE BUFFET

We delight in both cookouts and picnics but prefer picnics when the character of the food is delicate. Cooking in the organized convenience of our own kitchen, we can provide a variety of imaginative foods for our outdoor guests.

Only rain and lack of planning can spoil the day — and insufficient food. Our one firm rule: Always take more food and refreshments than you think you will need. The great outdoors stimulates the appetite as well as the flow of conversation.

For our picnic, we suggest a choice of two spinach entrees. They are perfect picnic fare any time of the year. Paul's Picnic Pie is a delicious Italian-style rustic pie. Torta Milanese is equally delectable. Both are wonderful served piping hot, lukewarm, or at room temperature. Best of all, they can be carried directly from your kitchen to the picnic area. We use a plastic pie carrier to carry the pie. You can also place the pie on a towel to prevent breaking the fragile rim of dough. For the torta, heat and wrap it immediately in heavy foil and cover with newspaper or place it in an insulated container to retain the heat.

Assorted beverages and white wine stay chilled if placed in an insulated picnic container packed with ice. The ice can be used in other ways: Plop some cubes into drinks, and when the remaining cubes melt, use the water for cleaning up.

This menu can double as a spur-of-the-moment party if you keep Paul's Picnic Pie and the finger-food sweets in the freezer; the other items can be obtained on a quick trip to the market.

Recipes for the finger-food sweets appear in the Exotic Curry and Chutney Buffet.

THE TABLE SETTINGS

This is an outdoor, casual picnic buffet for which knife and fork are required. Serve everything on a table; or if seated on the lawn, serve on a tablecloth or quilt.

Centerpiece.

The Basket of Fresh Fruits becomes an edible centerpiece.

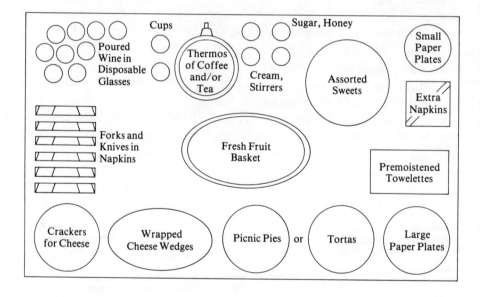

TIMETABLE

Three Days Before the Picnic. Both entrées are designed to be as easy as pie and can be made up to three days before serving, stored in the refrigerator, then served at room temperature or warmed. Paul's Picnic Pie is a specialty that we serve for many kinds of meals, so we usually keep several on hand in the freezer. When needed, we thaw the pie quickly in our microwave oven, then heat in a conventional oven to restore crispness. The torta should not be frozen.

We also keep assorted sweets on hand in the freezer, such as the Sunshine Squares and Black Bottom Cups, and in airtight tins we keep Macadamia Nut Candy Mauna Kea, Creamy Caramels with Walnuts, and our favorite jumbo Medjool dates.

Two Days Before the Picnic. Prepare the sweets, if not frozen, and wrap them individually in squares of plastic wrap for easy serving at the picnic. Store as described in the recipes.

The Day Before the Picnic. Prepare the pie or thaw if frozen. Pack the fruits and the crackers or bread. Wrap individual wedge-shaped servings of cheese in plastic wrap and refrigerate to be packed in the insulated container the next day (they will be at room temperature by serving time—the only temperature at which cheese should be served). Chill the wine and ready all other necessary equipment. Allow yourself the luxury of planning in advance and pack everything you can the night before; make a list of other items that need to be packed at the last minute.

The Day of the Picnic. Prepare the coffee and tea; pour into thermos bottles. Heat the pie or torta and pack as described in the introduction. If frozen, thaw the finger-food sweets. Check and pack the rest of the items.

All set? Check against our picnic checklist (which replaces the Countdown) and make sure you have everything you need.

PICNIC CHECKLIST

Equipment

    Insulated carrier with ice for wines, juices, and other refreshments
    Thermos bottles for coffee and tea
    Picnic cloth or quilts on which to serve food
    Cushions for sitting
    Plastic wine glasses
    Wine bottle openers, can opener
    Paper plates (large for main course, small for dessert and cheese)

Forks for entrée
Small knives and forks for fruit (optional)
Serrated knife for cutting torta
Server for pie or torta
Napkins
Baskets for fruit, cheese wedges, crackers or French bread, sweets
Knife for cutting French bread
Premoistened towelettes
Paper towels (to dip in melted ice for cleanup)
Bug repellent
Sunglasses
Sweaters

Food

Wine, juices, and other refreshments
Paul's Picnic Pie or Torta Milanese
Cheeses
Crackers or French bread
Fruit
Assorted sweets, in serving tins or individually wrapped to be
    heaped in a basket
Coffee, tea, cream, and sugar

RECIPES

PAUL'S PICNIC PIE

The Crust

Super-Flaky Pastry (see Recipes index), or use your favorite recipe
    for a two-crust 9-inch pie
1 egg, beaten, for glaze

The Filling

3 medium onions, minced
2 tablespoons olive oil
1 tablespoon butter
2 pounds fresh spinach leaves, washed, stemmed, and finely
    chopped, or 2 (10 ounces *each*) packages frozen chopped

spinach, thawed and squeezed of all excess moisture
¾ pound cooked ham, finely diced
1½ cups freshly grated Parmesan cheese
1 cup ricotta cheese
4 large eggs, beaten
1¼ teaspoons freshly ground black pepper
⅛ teaspoon freshly grated nutmeg or ground mace

Prepare the pastry dough and set aside.

To make the filling, sauté the onions in the olive oil and butter in a large heavy skillet over medium heat about five minutes, stirring often, until the onions are transparent. Blend in the spinach. (If you are using fresh spinach, place in a saucepan without additional water. Cover and cook for 6 minutes. Cool and squeeze of all excess moisture.) Cool the mixture to lukewarm. Mix in the ham, Parmesan, ricotta, eggs, pepper, and nutmeg or mace. Taste and adjust seasonings. Set aside until ready to fill the pastry shell.

Preheat the oven to 425°. To make the crust, roll out a little more than half the pastry dough on a lightly floured surface into a circle about 12 inches in diameter. Trim the uneven edges and reserve the trimmings for making the pastry "leaves." Ease the pastry into a 9½-inch, deep-dish pie plate (ours is Pyrex), taking care not to stretch the dough; gently press against the bottom and sides of the pan, leaving a ½-inch overhang. Turn the filling into the pastry-lined pan.

Roll out the remaining pastry into a circle about 10 inches in diameter. Trim the uneven edges and reserve the trimmings for the "leaves." Fit the crust over the filling. Trim the *top* crust even with the edge of the pie plate. Fold up the edges of the lower crust to form an even ½-inch-high rim around the pie plate. Seal all around by fluting with your fingers or the handle of a wooden spoon, or by pressing with the tines of a fork. Brush the entire surface of the crust with the beaten egg. With a thin, sharp knife, make a ¼-inch steam vent in the center of the crust. Bake in the center of the oven for 20 minutes.

Meanwhile, roll out the excess dough and make some leaves (directions appear in Garnishes appendix under Pastry Leaves and Flowers). Remove the pie from the oven, arrange the leaves around the steam vent to disguise but not cover it, and brush the leaves with the remaining egg glaze. Fold a strip of foil around the rim of the pie to prevent it from overbrowning. Return the pie to the oven for 20 minutes longer to finish baking. Cool on a rack for at least 20 minutes before cutting. Serve warm.

To Prepare in Advance. This pie can be baked up to three days ahead. Cool, then store, loosely covered, in the refrigerator. It also freezes well. Thaw completely, then reheat, uncovered, at 300° for about 20 minutes or until warm through.

TORTA MILANESE
For 16 Servings

2 pounds puff pastry purchased from bakery or 3 packages (10 ounces *each*) Pepperidge Farm frozen patty shells thawed

2 eggs, for egg wash

¼ cup freshly grated Parmesan cheese

¾ pound natural Swiss cheese, sliced

12 ounces baked ham, or 8 to 10 ounces domestic prosciutto, thinly sliced

8 ounces canned whole pimientos, opened flat, rinsed, and drained

The Spinach Layer

3 packages (10 ounces *each*) frozen chopped spinach, thawed and squeezed of all excess moisture

3 tablespoons minced chives or scallion tops

1 teaspoon salt
¼ teaspoon freshly ground black pepper
¼ teaspoon freshly grated nutmeg

The Egg Layer
2 tablespoons butter or margarine
Pinch each dried oregano, marjoram, thyme, and basil, or ½ teaspoon Italian herb seasoning
12 eggs
¼ cup heavy cream, half-and-half, or milk
½ teaspoon salt

To make the bottom crust, stack 13 of the patty shells on a lightly floured surface, and press down firmly with your hands to form one large patty. Flour the top and bottom of the pastry well, and roll out to a large circle that measures 17 inches, ½ inch larger around than is necessary to fit the bottom and to line the sides of a 10-inch spring-form pan. Use more flour if needed to prevent the dough from sticking to the rolling pin. Ease the pastry into the pan and gently press against the bottom and sides, leaving a ½-inch overhang. Separate one egg and lightly beat the white; reserve the yolk for the egg layer. With a pastry brush, brush the entire inside surface of the pastry, including the overhang, with the beaten white. This will "waterproof" your pastry and prevent it from becoming soggy when the filling is added. Refrigerate the pastry-lined pan if you do not intend filling immediately.

Preheat the oven to 425°. To assemble the torta, evenly sprinkle the bottom of the prepared shell with half the Parmesan. Top with a layer of half the sliced Swiss cheese and half the ham or prosciutto.

To make the spinach layer, mix the spinach with the chives, salt, pepper, and nutmeg. Spread it evenly over the ham or prosciutto. Top with the pimientos.

To make the egg layer, melt the butter with the herbs in a medium-large skillet (Teflon is perfect for this). Whisk the eggs with the extra yolk from the wash used for the pastry and the cream, half-and-half, or milk until thoroughly blended. Pour the mixture into the sizzling herb butter. Cook until set but still soft and creamy, like scrambled eggs. Layer over the pimientos. Top with the remaining ham or prosciutto, followed by the remaining Swiss cheese and Parmesan.

To make the top crust, set the remaining 5 patty shells on a lightly floured surface. Shape into a large patty. Flour the top and bottom well, and roll into a circle 11 inches in diameter. Ease the crust over the filling. Fold up the edges of the lower crust to form an even roll around the inside ring of the pan. Beat the remaining egg and brush over the entire surface of the torta to turn it beautifully golden as it bakes. With a thin, sharp knife, make several small cuts in the top pastry for steam vents. (We use fancy truffle cutters to do the job simply because we have them. We seldom have truffles, however.) Place the pan on a square piece of aluminum foil and bring the sides up to catch the butter that may leak out during baking.

Bake for 10 minutes, then lower the heat to 400° and continue baking for 45 minutes longer until the top is golden brown. Cool on a rack for at least 30 minutes before removing the spring-form side.

The best way to slice the torta is with an electric carving knife before taking it on your picnic. Or use a serrated knife—it won't crush the layers. Replace the spring-form sides of the pan. Serve warm or at room temperature.

To Prepare in Advance. Once baked and cooled, the torta may be stored in the refrigerator up to three days. We do not recommend freezing because the egg layer does not freeze particularly well.

BASKET OF FRESH FRUITS

Wash and arrange in a shallow basket an assortment of seasonal fruits from the following list. Avoid fragile and perishable fruits, such as berries. Summer-Fall: grapes, apricots, plums, nectarines or peaches, cherries. Winter-Spring: bananas, apples, tangerines, pears.

To Prepare in Advance. Arrange the fruits up to 12 hours in advance and store in a cool place.

BASKET OF WRAPPED CHEESE WEDGES

Choose a variety of at least three cheeses. Our choice would include a perfectly ripened Brie, a fine Cheddar, and one unusual cheese. Cut into 2-ounce portions and wrap securely in plastic wrap. Wrap at least two varieties of crackers, plain and lightly seasoned, six to a package. Pack cheese and crackers in a noncrushable container and keep in a cool place. Arrange with cheese spreaders in a basket. Serve at room temperature for best flavor.

To Prepare in Advance. The cheeses can be packed the night before and stored in the refrigerator. Remove from the refrigerator at least 2 hours before serving.

ENCORES

Why not picnic on the leftover goodies in your car on the way home? If you'd rather not do any snacking, the leftover pie or torta can be reheated once you are home. It should be eaten within two days. Store leftover sweets as directed in the recipes. Refrigerate tightly wrapped cheeses. Eat them within a week.

ITALIAN SUMMERTIME BUFFET

Menu

Bellini Punch

Bagna Cauda with Raw Vegetables

Turkey Tonnato

Soave or Verdicchio

Cannelloni di Melanzane

Prosciutto and Melon Platter

Sliced Tomatoes and Cheese with
Fresh Basil Dressing

Minted Watermelon Cups

Garlic and Parsley Bread Ring

Orange Slices in Liqueur

Ricotta Cheese Pie in a
Macaroon Crust

Sambuca Liqueur with
Roasted Coffee Beans

Coffee and Tea

LAVISH ITALIAN SUMMERTIME BUFFET

This lovely mélange of Mediterranean dishes is one of the most exciting buffets we've ever served. It is Italian at its most elegant. You'll find no pasta here, but pasta dishes appear on other pages.

The Bellini, a combination of champagne with puréed peaches, was invented at Harry's Bar in Venice. We made one change in creating our punch: We dice the peaches. Bagna Cauda makes a mystifying, but highly satisfying, chafing-dish dip. Your guests will taste and keep right on tasting, trying to identify the ingredients that make up this suave mixture.

For the Tonnato we have substituted Turkey breast for the traditional cold braised veal in Vitello Tonnato because it is more readily available. The tuna sauce is subtle, and the combination of flavors still makes this one of the most epicurean of all buffet dishes. The cannelloni with their eggplant-cheese filling are reminiscent of the Melanzane Nostra served at the La Scala restaurant in Beverly Hills, California.

The orange slices are primarily a dessert for light eaters and may be served with or without the pie. The Ricotta Cheese Pie recipe is by Arthur Gold and Robert Fizdale and originally appeared in *Vogue* magazine. The macaroons used are available at gourmet specialty shops and are expensive, but they are worth the price in flavor and after-dinner fun. At one of our buffets Katrina Cord, who had made the pie and brought along the macaroon wrappers, showed us a party game, fully described at the end of this chapter. It helped light up our evening. May you have the same kind of spectacular evening when you serve this buffet. *Buòn appetito!*

THE TABLE SETTINGS

This is a lavish, single-line buffet. Knife and fork are required; silverware and napkins are placed at preset tables. Punch, appetizer, desserts, and beverages are served separately.

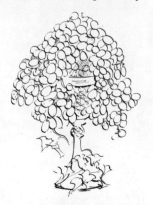

Centerpieces

Buffet Table. Grapes and ivy. In a shallow basket, mound an assortment of purple and red grape clusters. Intersperse with small pots of English ivy. A quick spray with a nonstick cooking spray will make your arrangement glisten.

Dining Tables. Grapes. For each table, drape clusters of green grapes from a tall, footed vase. For easy draping, tie together the stems of four bunches of grapes, drape over the side of the vase, and mound other clusters on top. Stud the centerpiece with nontoxic garden flowers just before guests arrive. Include a pair of grape shears for guests to snip off clusters for convenient nibbling.

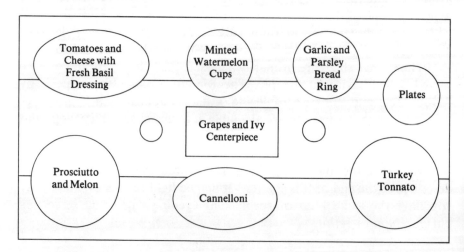

TIMETABLE

Two Months Before the Party. The component parts of the cannelloni can be made ahead and frozen separately. In fact, crêpes, Diana's Quick Basic Brown Sauce, and béchamel may be staples you already have on hand in your freezer. Or the completely assembled dish may be frozen according to our directions in the recipe.

Three Days Before the Party. Cook the turkey; chill it in the braising liquid until ready to slice. The pie, salad dressing, and Bagna Cauda may also be prepared.

The Day Before the Party. Prepare the fresh vegetable dippers for the Bagna Cauda and store as described in the recipe. Make the sauce for the turkey. Prepare the orange dessert and chill in the serving bowl. If the cannelloni have been frozen, thaw overnight in the refrigerator. Make the ice ring and chill the champagne for the punch.

The Morning of the Party. Peel and chop the peaches for the punch and chill in a solution of Fruit Fresh or lemon juice to prevent darkening. Prepare the watermelon cups, garnish with mint, and chill, right on a serving tray if possible. Prepare the bread ring for baking and keep chilled. At least 6 hours before serving, layer the tonnato sauce and sliced turkey and chill. Up to 4 hours before serving, prepare the salad, garnish, cover, and chill. Arrange the Turkey Tonnato on the serving platter, garnish, and chill. Prepare the prosciutto and melon and chill.

COUNTDOWN

1 hour before guests arrive:	Arrange basket of cut vegetables for dip.
	Remove cannelloni from refrigerator and top with cheese for baking.
30 minutes before guests arrive:	Place Turkey Tonnato and salad on buffet table.
15 minutes before guests arrive:	Unmold ice ring and place in punch bowl with peaches and crème de cassis.
	Prepare coffee and tea.
5 minutes before guests arrive:	Reheat dip gently, whisking until smooth. Place in chafing dish or fondue pot.

As guests arrive:	Add champagne to punch bowl.
40 minutes before serving:	Bake bread ring (375° for 30 minutes or 350° for 35 minutes).
30 minutes before serving:	Bake cannelloni (350° for 20 to 30 minutes) until it bubbles.
10 minutes before serving:	Remove bread ring from oven; let cool.
5 minutes before serving:	Turn bread onto serving plate. Set out watermelon cups and prosciutto-wrapped melon. Garnish cannelloni with parsley and place on buffet table. Announce dinner.

RECIPES

BELLINI PUNCH

3 large ripe peaches
2 bottles (fifths) champagne, chilled
¼ cup crème de cassis (black currant liqueur)
Lemon Ice Ring or Minted Ice Ring (see Ice Rings in Garnishes appendix)

Drop the peaches one at a time in boiling water to cover for 30 seconds. Cool in cold water. Peel and remove pits, then dice finely.

Just before serving, combine peaches and chilled champagne in a pitcher or in a punchbowl with an ice ring. Sweeten to taste with the crème de cassis. Serve immediately.

To Prepare in Advance. Mix diced peaches with Fruit Fresh, a powdered ascorbic acid (vitamin C) available in most supermarkets. It is used in home canning to prevent fruit from darkening without affecting the flavor. Follow package directions.

BAGNA CAUDA WITH RAW VEGETABLES
The Vegetable Basket

2 carrots, cut in ⅛-inch sticks
6 stalks celery, cut in ⅛-inch sticks

½ head cauliflower, separated into flowerets
6 radishes, decoratively cut
½ green bell pepper, cut in slender sticks
½ red bell pepper, cut in slender sticks
½ small jícama (see *Note*), cut in ¼-inch sticks (optional)
3 large mushrooms, cleaned and cut in quarters through the stems
8 bread sticks (we prefer the Grissini type)

The Bagna Cauda
1 cup heavy cream (whipping cream)
1½ tablespoons butter
½ clove garlic, pressed
¼ (2-ounce) can flat anchovy fillets, drained and mashed, or 1½
   teaspoons anchovy paste
¼ teaspoon dried thyme leaves, crumbled
¼ teaspoon dried oregano, crumbled
Dash white pepper
⅛ teaspoon salt or more, to taste

To Decorate
1 large head curly lettuce
Assorted garden flowers

Note: Jícama, a turnip-looking tuber with a sweet taste reminiscent of apples and water chestnuts, makes a delicious low-calorie "dipper." It's Mexican, not Italian, but who cares?

Prepare the vegetables; place all but the mushrooms in a large bowl of ice water to crisp for at least 1 hour. Wrap the mushrooms in damp paper towels and store in the refrigerator. When the vegetables are crisp, pat dry. Use the leaves of the curly lettuce to completely line a shallow rustic basket or serving platter. Arrange all the vegetables and bread sticks decoratively on top of the leaves. Fill the hollows with garden-fresh flowers.

To make the Bagna Cauda, simmer the cream slowly in a heavy enamel or stainless-steel skillet until it is reduced to half its original volume. This will take from 10 to 30 minutes, depending on the quantity you are making. Stir the cream constantly toward the end of the cooking time to prevent scorching.

Meanwhile, melt the butter in a small saucepan over very low heat. Stir in the garlic and let heat very gently for about 5 minutes. Do not let it burn. Stir in the mashed anchovies or anchovy paste, herbs, and seasonings. Simmer slowly for 5 to 10 minutes until smooth. Very gradually beat in the reduced cream and heat just *to* the boiling point without boiling. Taste for seasoning. Add more salt and pepper, if needed.

Serve the Bagna Cauda in an earthenware dish or a fondue pot over a low flame, accompanied by the assortment of crisp vegetables.

To Prepare in Advance. The cut vegetables may be wrapped in damp paper towels and placed in a large plastic bag for refrigerator storage. They will stay crisp and fresh at least 24 hours. Arrange the vegetables in a serving basket no more than 2 hours in advance. Cover with damp paper towels and store in the refrigerator or a cool place. The Bagna Cauda may also be made ahead. Cool to room temperature, then refrigerate, covered, up to three days. Do not worry if it separates. At serving time gently reheat while beating vigorously with a whisk until it is smooth and creamy again.

TURKEY TONNATO

The Turkey

1 whole turkey breast (about 4 pounds), split and boned (see *Note*)
3 cups chicken or turkey broth
2 cups dry vermouth or white wine
3 stalks celery, sliced
2 carrots, sliced
1 large onion, chopped
2 medium cloves garlic, cut in half

The Tonnato Sauce

Broth from braising the turkey
1 (3½-ounce) can oil-packed tuna, drained
6 canned anchovy fillets, rinsed and drained, or 1½ teaspoons anchovy paste
1 tablespoon freshly squeezed lemon juice
Salt to taste
Cayenne or white pepper to taste
¾ cup heavy cream (whipping cream)

The Garnish

Parsley
1 tablespoon capers, rinsed and well drained
2 to 3 lemons, thinly sliced

1 (2-ounce) can rolled anchovies with capers, drained
A Lemon Rose (see Garnishes appendix), several daisies, or other
flowers

For 16 Servings. Recipe may be doubled, but 1½ times the amount of
turkey (6 pounds) will be sufficient. It is best to double the sauce. You'll
be glad to have the extra on hand.

For 32 Servings. A triple recipe will be sufficient. Serve on two large
round platters.

Note: The breast should be *boned but not skinned.* You may ask the
butcher to do this for you, but it isn't difficult to do yourself. Split the
breast along the breastbone. Use your forefinger to loosen the meat
from the bones along the rib cage. Then use a small knife to finish the
job. One at a time, lay the boned breast halves, skin side down on your
work surface. Roll into a neat roll, wrapping the skin tightly around the
meat to form a long sausage-like roll. Wrap in several layers of cheesecloth, and secure the ends of the cheesecloth with string.

Place the rolled breast in a saucepan just large enough to hold it
comfortably without crowding. Add the broth, wine, vegetables and
garlic. Partially cover the pot with a lid and bring to a boil. Lower the
heat and simmer for about 1 hour until the turkey reaches an internal
temperature of 165° when tested with a meat thermometer. Chill the
breast in the broth overnight.

The next day remove the breast from the stock and the cheesecloth, reserving the stock. Discard the skin. Slice the turkey meat (an
electric carving knife is ideal for this) in even ⅜-inch slices. Refrigerate.

To make the sauce, strain the braising liquid and skim away most
of the fat from the surface. Boil the liquid in a saucepan over high heat
until it is reduced to ½ cup. The flavor will be highly concentrated.
Cool. Place the broth in a blender or food processor with the tuna,
anchovy fillets, lemon juice, salt, and cayenne or white pepper. Blend
until puréed and pour into a mixing bowl. Taste for seasoning. The mixture should be overseasoned because the flavor will be diluted when the
cream is added. Whip the cream only until it holds a soft shape—do not
beat until stiff. Fold the whipped cream into the sauce until very smooth.

To assemble, place one layer of sliced turkey in a large shallow
glass dish or stainless-steel pan and spoon sauce over to cover. Repeat
the layers until you have used up all the turkey and sauce. Cover and

refrigerate for at least 6 hours to allow the flavor of the sauce to permeate the turkey.

Within 4 hours of serving, gently lift the turkey slices from the sauce and arrange on a large serving dish around a cluster of parsley sprigs. Spoon sauce over the meat and sprinkle with the capers.

Wreathe with thin slices of lemon; top with rolled anchovies. For a final touch, add the lemon rose, fresh daisies, or other small flowers.

To Prepare in Advance. The turkey may be cooked and chilled in the broth three days ahead. Make the sauce and combine with the sliced turkey no less than 6 hours or no more than 24 hours ahead.

CANNELLONI DI MELANZANE

The Béchamel Sauce
4 tablespoons butter or margarine
¼ cup all-purpose flour
2 cups cold milk, or 1½ cups milk and ½ cup chicken broth
½ teaspoon salt
½ teaspoon sugar
¼ teaspoon freshly grated nutmeg
Dash of cayenne or white pepper

The Filling
¼ cup minced onion
3 tablespoons olive oil
1 small clove garlic, pressed
¾ pound eggplant, peeled and cut into ½-inch cubes
½ teaspoon dried oregano
Pinch dried thyme, crumbled
½ teaspoon salt
⅛ teaspoon freshly ground black pepper
¼ cup freshly grated Parmesan cheese

8 five- or six-inch crêpes (see Recipes index)
¼ pound Fontina or Gruyère cheese, thinly sliced
½ cup Diana's Quick Basic Brown Sauce (recipe follows)
¼ cup freshly grated Parmesan cheese

The Garnish
1 tablespoon minced parsley

For 16 Cannelloni. Recipe may be doubled. Serve in a baking dish large enough to hold the cannelloni without their touching.

For 32 Cannelloni. Double the recipe and make it twice. (Don't quadruple in one skillet.) You will need two baking dishes sufficiently large to hold 16 cannelloni each without their touching.

To make the béchamel sauce, melt the butter in a heavy skillet or saucepan. Stir in the flour and cook over medium heat, stirring constantly for about 3 minutes to make a *roux*. Do not let the flour brown. Remove pan from the heat and whisk in the cold milk all at once. Return to heat, add the chicken broth and seasonings, and whisk the sauce over medium heat until boiling and thickened. Remove from heat, cover with plastic wrap to prevent a skin from forming, and set aside until needed. Makes 2 cups.

To make the filling, sauté the onion in the olive oil in a large heavy skillet until the the onion is transparent. Add the garlic and sauté for 1 minute, then add the eggplant, oregano, and thyme. Cook slowly for 20 to 30 minutes, stirring often, until the eggplant is tender. Remove from heat and stir in the salt, pepper, ¼ cup Parmesan, and ⅓ cup of the béchamel sauce. Transfer to a blender or food processor and blend until smooth.

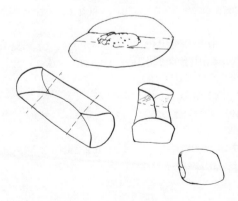

To assemble, divide the filling into 8 portions. Place 1 portion in the center of each crêpe and fold in the four sides to enclose the filling (it will look like an envelope). Place the cannelloni about ½-inch apart, seam side down, in a 9x13-inch buttered baking dish. For ease in serving, the rolls should not touch each other. Top each with a slice of Fontina or Gruyère cheese of the same size. Pour the remaining sauce in the spaces between the cannelloni, followed by a drizzle of brown sauce. The cannelloni should still be visible. Sprinkle with ¼ cup Parmesan.

Bake at 350° for 20 minutes (if at room temperature) or 30 minutes (if chilled). Garnish with chopped parsley.

To Prepare in Advance. The entire dish may be completely assembled and frozen two months before the party. Do not top with the sliced cheese until after the cannelloni have thawed and you are ready to bake (freezing has an adverse effect on cheese). Or if you already have béchamel sauce, brown sauce, and crêpes on hand in your freezer, thaw overnight in the refrigerator. On the day before the party, prepare the entire dish ready for the oven. Cover tightly with foil or plastic wrap and store in the refrigerator. Bring to room temperature before baking.

DIANA'S QUICK BASIC BROWN SAUCE

¼ pound (1 stick) butter or margarine
1 large onion, chopped
2 carrots, chopped fine
¼ cup parsley (leaves or stems), chopped
¼ teaspoon dried thyme, crumbled
1 large clove garlic, cut in half and flattened
½ cup all-purpose flour
3 (10¾ ounces *each*) cans condensed beef broth or bouillon
3 cups water
1 cup mixed wine (we use ¼ cup sherry or Madeira, ⅓ cup dry
    white wine, and a red burgundy to make 1 cup)
1 bay leaf
1 stalk celery, chopped
2 tablespoons tomato paste
1 whole clove
½ teaspoon beef extract, or 1½ teaspoons Maggi seasoning
Black pepper to taste

Melt the butter in a 3- to 4-quart heavy-bottomed saucepan. Add the next five ingredients and cook, stirring often, until they start to brown. Stir in the flour and continue cooking, stirring often, until the mixture (or *roux*) turns a light brown color. Be careful not to scorch the flour or it will not thicken the sauce properly. When the flour is light brown, stir in all the remaining ingredients. Bring to a boil, then lower the heat and simmer gently for 40 minutes, stirring occasionally. Strain the sauce before using. Makes 1 quart.

To Prepare in Advance. It is very nice to have this brown sauce on hand in your freezer to use whenever a French brown sauce or sauce espagnole is called for. We freeze it in ice-cube trays and then transfer the frozen cubes to a plastic bag. The required amount can be thawed very quickly. Use the cubes to enrich gravies.

PROSCIUTTO AND MELON PLATTER
½ ripe cantaloupe or honeydew (or a combination or both)
2 ounces thinly sliced prosciutto, domestic or imported

To Serve
12 frilled cocktail picks

For 32 Servings. A triple recipe will be sufficient.

Cut the melon flesh into twelve 1-inch cubes. Wrap each cube in a strip of prosciutto and secure with a frilled pick. Arrange on a serving plate. Serve chilled or at room temperature.

To Prepare in Advance. Prepare within 4 hours of serving. Chill to within 1 hour of serving, then bring to room temperature.

SLICED TOMATOES AND CHEESE
WITH FRESH BASIL DRESSING
½ pound packaged sliced mozzarella, Muenster, or Monterey Jack cheese
4 large ripe tomatoes, sliced ¼-inch thick

The Dressing

>2 tablespoons red wine vinegar
>⅓ cup olive oil
>1 medium clove garlic
>2 tablespoons minced fresh basil (see *Note*)
>1 tablespoon minced parsley
>¼ teaspoon salt
>⅛ teaspoon dry mustard
>Freshly ground black pepper, to taste

The Garnish

>½ cup pitted black olives
>Sprigs of basil or parsley

Note: Two teaspoons of crumbled, dry sweet basil may be substituted when fresh basil is not available, but it will impart an entirely different flavor.

Cut the cheese slices in half crosswise into squares, then diagonally to form triangles. Arrange attractively on a shallow plate or serving dish by overlapping the triangles of cheese and tomatoes. Scatter the olives on top.

To make the dressing, combine all ingredients in a blender or food processor and blend. Store in the refrigerator if not using immediately. Bring to room temperature when ready to serve.

Before serving, pour the dressing evenly over the tomatoes and cheese and garnish with fresh basil or parsley sprigs.

To Prepare in Advance. The dressing may be stored in the refrigerator for three days. Bring to room temperature before serving. Arrange the tomatoes and cheese on the platter within 4 hours of serving and cover with plastic wrap. Chill. Remove from refrigerator, add dressing, and garnish at least 1 hour before serving to bring to room temperature.

MINTED WATERMELON CUPS

¼ to ½ large ripe watermelon
8 sprigs mint

Use a melon-ball maker to make 5 to 7 balls per person. The number depends on the size of your serving dishes. We like to use small soufflé dishes or ramekins. They not only look attractive but help contain the juices. Garnish each dish with a sprig of mint and chill.

To Prepare in Advance. Chill and garnish in the serving dishes up to 8 hours before serving.

GARLIC AND PARSLEY BREAD RING

For up to 16 people
10 tablespoons (1¼ sticks) butter
2 cloves garlic, pressed
¼ cup chopped parsley
3 packages (8 ounces *each*) Pillsbury Butterflake Refrigerator Rolls

Melt the butter in a small saucepan. Stir in the garlic and cook very slowly for 2 to 3 minutes. Remove from heat and cool slightly. Add the chopped parsley. Dip the butterflake rolls one at a time in the seasoned butter and arrange them at random in a bundt pan or 12-cup ring mold. (Do not use an angel food cake pan or the butter will leak out during baking.)
Bake at 375° for 30 minutes. Let rest in the pan for 5 minutes, then turn out onto a serving platter. Serve immediately.

To Prepare in Advance. Prepare up to the point of baking and refrigerate up to 12 hours ahead. Bake just before serving.

ORANGE SLICES IN LIQUEUR

8 medium navel oranges, or oranges in season
Zest (yellow peel) of 1 medium lemon, chopped
2 tablespoons sugar
2 tablespoons orange-flavored liqueur (such as Triple Sec, Cointreau, or Grand Marnier), or freshly squeezed lemon juice

For 32 Servings. Since this is primarily a dessert for light eaters or an accompaniment to the pie, a triple recipe in a large bowl will be sufficient.

Cut the ends off the oranges. Stand them on end, one at a time, and with a small, sharp knife cut the peel away, using a downward stroke. Be sure to remove all the white pith. Slice the oranges crosswise in ¼-inch-thick slices. Remove the seeds if you are not using navel oranges. Place in a serving bowl and sprinkle with lemon zest, sugar, and liqueur or lemon juice. Turn gently to blend flavorings and refrigerate at least 3 hours. Serve chilled.

To Prepare in Advance. Prepare up to 24 hours in advance, cover, and store in the refrigerator until serving time.

RICOTTA CHEESE PIE IN A MACAROON CRUST
The Crust
    16 to 18 individually wrapped double macaroons (Amaretti di Saronno, Lazzaroni brand), enough to make 1½ cups of crumbs
    6 tablespoons (¾ stick) butter

The Filling
    ½ cup seedless raisins or dried currants
    5 tablespoons orange-flavored liqueur (such as Aurum, Cointreau, or Grand Marnier), or orange juice
    1½ cups (12 ounces) ricotta cheese
    1 cup superfine sugar
    5 egg yolks
    1 whole egg
    Zest of 1 lemon, grated
    Pinch of salt
    A few sprinkles of cinnamon

For 32 Servings. Make only three pies. Some guests will opt for no dessert or very thin slices or may prefer just the orange slices.

At least 24 hours ahead, put raisins or currants in liqueur or juice to soak.

Crush the macaroons to make very fine crumbs, either with a rolling pin—or, infinitely easier—in a food processor, using a steel blade. Mix in melted butter until crumbs stick together. Spread mixture over sides and bottom of a 9- or 10-inch pie plate and put into shape. Or shape by pressing an identical pie pan down over the crumbs; chill for 1 hour or bake at 300° for 15 minutes, then let cool for 30 minutes.

Meanwhile, prepare fillings: In a mixing bowl combine all ingredients, except raisins or currants, and stir until smooth. Stir in drained currants (reserving their liquid for another use) and fill pie shell. Bake 1 hour at 350° or until filling is golden and firm. Serve at room temperature, cool, or after several hours in the refrigerator.

To Prepare in Advance. Store in the refrigerator up to three days. Do not freeze.

SAMBUCCA LIQUEUR WITH ROASTED COFFEE BEANS

This clear licorice syrup, known as "Rome's *dolce vita* liqueur," is made from elderberries and is a favorite Italian after-dinner liqueur. It is traditionally served in cordial glasses in which roasted coffee beans are set afloat, three to a glass. Take care with the coffee beans. If ingested, they may cause insomnia.

FLAMING AMARETTI WRAPPERS

If you don't buy the exquisite, paper-wrapped, imported macaroons called Amaretti di Saronno (Lazzaroni brand) for the Ricotta Cheese Pie, then buy some to serve with the coffee and/or liqueurs and end your evening with this flaming finale.

Here's how Katrina Cord instructed us at our party. Provide one macaroon wrapper per guest. Each wrapper should be rolled into a cylinder-shaped chimney, balanced on end in an ashtray, and the top end ignited. The flame will burn downward. When the flame reaches the bottom, the wrapper takes off, floating lightly toward the ceiling. The ashes float back down to earth when the wrapper stops smoldering and are easily captured in an ashtray.

It's an exciting, though short-lived, pastime. It is more fun when all the guests take turns lighting up. While you sip your caffé espresso and Sambucca, watch to see whose cylinder floats the highest—a lucky omen for that person—and relish the flaming spectacle to the end.

ENCORES

You'd best polish off the punch the same day—champagne loses its sparkle very quickly. Because most of this menu is served cold, the rest of the leftovers will keep beautifully and be just as delicious the next day. Simply arrange them attractively on fresh serving plates. The hot dishes, dip, cannelloni, and bread ring suffer minimally by gentle reheating. To rebeautify the Turkey Tonnato, spoon off most of the sauce and rearrange the slices on a fresh serving dish. Spoon the sauce over the top and sprinkle with well-drained capers and chopped fresh parsley. A sprinkling of fresh parsley does wonders for almost anything.

Mexican Fiesta Buffet

Menu

Puerto Vallarta Punch

Cacahuetes Picantes

Guacamole María Theresa

Mexican Beer or

Full-Bodies White or Red Wine

Chicken Mole in Foil

Arroz Verde

Chiles Rellenos de Picadillo

Fiesta Fruit Banderillas

Mango Sherbet

Iced Margarita Soufflé

Coffee and Tea

MEXICAN FIESTA BUFFET

A Mexican Fiesta is *the* summer patio buffet to give, with the decorations, menu, mingling of guests, music, and conversation all contributing toward an atmosphere every bit as festive as an evening in the plaza of an old Mexican village.

One of the main courses (there are two) for the Mexican Fiesta Buffet is the historic Chicken Mole. For those who like fashioning things, we include two ways to package the mole in foil: One is simple; one is not. However, you may also serve the mole, topped with sauce and sprinkled with sesame seeds, over rice in a large serving dish. The other entree is a simple but special dish of meat-stuffed chiles from Puebra, Mexico. The menu is balanced with refreshing cubes of skewered chilled fruit and a light Mango Sherbet.

All true guacamole aficionados will be indebted to our friend, María Theresa. Appalled at our inauthentic molded version, for our next party she made guacamole Guadalajara style.

Chiles Rellenos is our version of a dish made to welcome us one Christmas at the Villa Santa Monica Hotel in San Miguel de Allende, Mexico. Elena, the hotel chef, used chiles poblanos (fat ones, or *gordos*), which she roasted over an open fire and then peeled. We have substituted canned whole chiles to make this astonishingly easy dish that never fails to get raves.

The skewered fruit is one of Paul's creations. The frilled skewers are named after the ornamental darts used in bull fights. When speared with fruit, they make a spectacular centerpiece and offer fruit for the taking. The centerpieces at the guests' tables, on the other hand, are in-season chiles, which you can use the next day to make pimiento jelly, chiles rellenos, spiced vinegar, and other dishes.

103

THE TABLE SETTINGS

This is a lavish, single-line, seated buffet. Knife and fork are required; silverware and napkins are on preset tables. Punch, appetizers, dessert, and beverages are served separately.

Centerpieces

Buffet Table. You will need a casaba melon, half a watermelon (cut crosswise), parsley, Fiesta Fruit Banderillas (see recipe in this section), a round serving platter, and fresh daisies or other nontoxic flowers. Slice an inch from the bottom (stem end) of the casaba melon so that it stands flat. Place in the center of the platter. Cut the watermelon in eight lengthwise slices. Arrange them to resemble the spokes of a wheel with the blunt ends touching the casaba. Insert sprigs of parsley between each spoke to completely cover the platter. Using an icepick or metal skewer, poke holes in a symmetrical pattern over the top half of the melon. Just before serving insert the fruit banderillas. Stud the

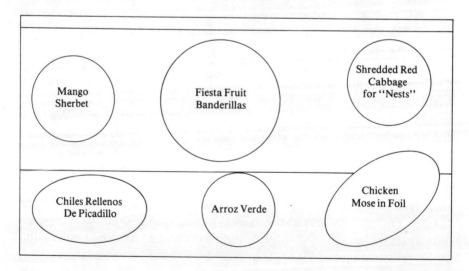

parsley with daisies. The centerpiece can be assembled the morning of the party, with the exception of the parsley and fresh flowers. Cover with a damp tea towel and store in a cool, dark place.

Dining Tables. For each centerpiece, you will need 2 round baskets (one larger than the other); parsley; fresh flowers; and red, green, and yellow chile peppers. Make a wreath of the parsley around the perimeter of the larger basket. Stud with the flowers. In the smaller basket, heap in the peppers, piling them high in the center, and set within the larger basket. Spray with nonstick cooking spray to give the peppers a sheen. Arrange and set out the centerpieces within 2 hours of the party. Spray the parsley with a mister to keep it fresh and moist.

TIMETABLE

The foil "chickens" or hearts in which to serve the mole and the frilled skewers can be made anytime convenient for you. Store the foil chickens on a tray out of harm's way and the skewers upright in a glass.

The Mango Sherbet and the ice ring can be frozen up to three weeks before the party. If you wish, you can prepare the peanuts two weeks ahead. At the same time, freeze the soufflé; otherwise, prepare it two days before the party, along with the punch and the mole sauce, and refrigerate.

The Day Before the Party. Prepare the chicken, chiles rellenos, and puréed vegetables for the rice and refrigerate. If you have not prepared the peanuts earlier, do so now. If frozen, thaw the soufflé in the refrigerator overnight. Scoop servings of sherbet into ramekins and return to freezer.

The Morning of the Party. Within 4 hours of serving, cut the fruit and thread on skewers. Keep them fresh as described in the recipe. Prepare all garnishes (the lime slices with flowers for the sherbet and the scallions for chiles rellenos), cover with damp towels, and set them out near your work area. Three hours ahead, make the guacamole dip. Shred red cabbage if you are using "nests" for the chicken mole. Place the chicken breasts and mole sauce in the packages, seal, and leave at room temperature.

COUNTDOWN

1 hour before guests arrive: Whip cream, garnish dessert, and chill.

	Set out the peanuts in serving bowls.
	Set out chiles rellenos to come to room temperature.
	Make the rice and place in crock-pot or foil to keep warm.
	Chill beer or wine on ice.
15 minutes before guests arrive:	Unmold ice ring, finish punch, and set out.
	Garnish and set out guacamole dip with corn chips or crackers.
	Place skewers of fruit in melon.
	Prepare coffee and tea.
15 minutes before serving:	Place chicken mole and chiles rellenos in oven at 350°.
5 minutes before serving:	Take out chicken mole and chiles rellenos. Top the latter with sour cream and return to the oven for 3 minutes together with the rice, if it is to be reheated in foil.
	Garnish the tray of sherbet and set out.
	Set out the chicken mole and red cabbage, if making nests.
	Transfer rice to serving bowl, if necessary.
	Take chiles rellenos out of oven and set out.
At serving time:	If serving chicken in foil, hand each guest a plate containing chicken set atop a red cabbage nest; otherwise, guests serve themselves.

RECIPES

PUERTO VALLARTA PUNCH

2 cups light rum
2 cups freshly squeezed, strained orange juice
½ cup freshly squeezed, strained lemon juice

½ cup freshly squeezed, strained lime juice
½ cup Orgeat syrup
½ cup Sweet and Sour Mix
½ cup Curaçao or Triple Sec
¼ cup dark rum (preferably Myer's label)
¼ cup grenadine
1 to 2 cups club soda, chilled

The Garnish

Fresh pineapple wedges
Strawberries
Mint sprigs
Minted Ice Ring (see Ice Rings in Garnishes appendix)

Combine all ingredients, except the club soda and garnish; chill thoroughly. Just before serving, add the fruit garnish and as much of the chilled club soda as you wish, to suit your taste. Serve in a pitcher with ice cubes, or double the recipe to serve in a punch bowl with the ice ring.

To Prepare in Advance. Combine all ingredients, except the club soda and garnish. Cover and keep chilled up to 48 hours. Just before serving, stir and add the club soda and fruit garnish.

CACAHUETES PICANTES
For 16 servings

3 tablespoons olive oil or butter (or a combination of both)
16 small dried red chile peppers, each about 1 inch long (see *Note*)
2 cloves garlic, pressed
2 (12 ounces *each*) cans "jumbo" roasted peanuts
1 teaspoon coarse salt (kosher salt)
1 teaspoon chili powder

Note: Many varieties of this chile, any of which will work fine, can be found at most markets.

Heat the olive oil and/or butter, chile peppers, and garlic in a heavy medium-size skillet for 1 or 2 minutes, stirring constantly to avoid scorching the chiles. Stir in the peanuts and transfer to a foil-lined (for easy cleanup) baking sheet and bake at 350° for 5 to 8 minutes or until lightly browned. Sprinkle with the salt and chili powder. Mix well and cool. Transfer to a storage container (we use glass jars), cover, and let mellow at room temperature for at least 24 hours before serving.

To Prepare in Advance. Store the peanuts in jars at room temperature up to two weeks or in the refrigerator up to three months. For best flavor, serve at room temperature.

GUACAMOLE MARÍA THERESA
    2 large or 3 medium ripe avocados
    ½ large onion, minced
    2 medium tomatoes, minced (do not skin)
    5 small fresh *chiles verdes* (see *Note*)
    1 to 1½ teaspoons salt

To Serve
    Tortilla chips

Note: Maria Theresa made this dip with very hot tiny green chiles bought in a Mexican grocery store. You can substitute canned jalapeno or any other fresh hot chile.

Remove the pits from the avocados. In a mixing bowl, mash the pulp and combine with the remaining ingredients, adjusting seasonings to taste. Transfer to a serving bowl and accompany with tortilla chips for dipping.

To Prepare in Advance. Make within 3 hours of serving. Press in the avocado pits to prevent the mixture from darkening; seal with plastic wrap. Remove pits before serving.

CHICKEN MOLE IN FOIL
For 16 servings

    16 chicken *suprèmes* with skin (8 breasts, split and boned)
    Vegetable oil for browning
    1 cup chicken broth

The Mole Sauce
    1 (8-ounce) can tomato sauce
    2 onions, coarsely chopped
    2 medium cloves garlic, pressed

1 (3½-ounce) bag slivered almonds
½ cup seedless raisins
½ cup chili powder
¼ cup crushed commercial corn chips, or 1 corn tortilla, torn in small pieces
3 tablespoons toasted sesame seeds (see *Note*)
2 tablespoons firmly packed chopped parsley
1 tablespoon smooth peanut butter
1 tablespoon Worcestershire sauce
2 teaspoons sugar
2 teaspoons salt
¾ teaspoon ground cinnamon
½ teaspoon ground cumin
½ teaspoon ground cloves
½ teaspoon ground coriander, or 2 tablespoons minced fresh *cilantro*
¼ teaspoon anise seed
¼ to ½ teaspoon freshly ground black pepper
1½ to 2 cups chicken broth
1½ ounces (1½ squares) unsweetened chocolate

To Garnish

About 2 tablespoons toasted sesame seeds (see *Note*)

To Serve

Arroz Verde (recipe follows)
½ head finely shredded red cabbage (to use as nests if the mole is served inside foil "chickens")

Note: To toast sesame seeds, place single layer in a foil pie tin. Toast at 350° for 5 to 7 minutes until lightly browned. Be careful not to let them burn.

For 8 Servings. For the sake of convenience make the sauce in the amount given for 16 servings. Freeze any extra for another occasion.

For 32 Servings. Double the sauce ingredients. Cook in two separate pans to avoid burning the sauce.

Dry the chicken well with paper towels. Heat about ⅛ inch of oil in a large skillet. Sauté the chicken *suprèmes* about six at a time (do not crowd them) until browned on both sides. Transfer to a large skillet with a lid. Repeat with the remaining chicken. Reserve the drippings.

Pour the 1 cup of chicken broth over the breasts, cover, and simmer slowly about 5 minutes until the breasts are almost, but not quite, done (they should be pink when cut in the center with a sharp knife). Pour off the broth and reserve for use in making the mole sauce. Let the breasts cool.

To make the sauce, pour off all but ¼ cup of the drippings from the skillet. In a large bowl combine all the sauce ingredients except the chocolate. Add the broth in which the breasts were cooked. Mix well. Place about one third of the mixture at a time in a blender or food processor and blend until almost smooth—the sauce should have some texture. Transfer the blended mixture to the skillet with the drippings. Bring to a boil, then lower the heat and, stirring often, simmer slowly for 30 minutes. Remove from heat. Chop the chocolate coarsely and place on top of the sauce. The heat from the sauce will melt the chocolate. When melted, stir into the sauce. Remove from heat. Taste for seasoning, adding more salt and pepper if needed. If the sauce seems too thick, thin it with more chicken broth.

Place one *suprème* inside each of the foil chickens you have made (directions follow). Spoon the sauce evenly among the packages. Sprinkle with sesame seeds and seal tightly. Bake the packages at 350° for 10 minutes. (If the breasts and sauce are not warm when placed in the oven, bake another 5 minutes.) Serve on a "nest" of shredded red cabbage.

To serve the chicken without the foil packages, place the chicken *suprèmes* and the sauce in a baking pan, cover with foil and bake in a 325° oven about 20 to 25 minutes. Arrange the breasts on top of the rice in a large serving dish. Spoon the sauce decoratively over the breasts, leaving some green rice visible. Sprinkle with sesame seeds.

To Prepare in Advance. The mole sauce can be made several days before the party. Or, both breasts and sauce can be prepared the day before. Cool separately, then fill the foil packages several hours before baking. Seal and leave at room temperature. Before serving, heat at 350° for 15 minutes.

FOIL PACKAGES FOR CHICKEN MOLE

There are two ways to prepare Chicken Mole in foil. The most practical method is in a package similar to the French way of serving veal chops *en papillote.* To do this with ease, brown the chicken and prepare the mole the day before your party and refrigerate. On the day of the party, prepare the foil packages and heat. The heart-shaped foil is simple to construct and has a classic appearance when served. Here is how:

1. For each serving, tear off one foot of 12-inch-wide, heavy-duty aluminum foil. Fold the square in half to form a triangle, shiny side out. (In place of foil, you could use the more traditional oiled cooking parchment.)

2. With a pencil, draw half of a wide heart, beginning and ending on the folded edge. Cut along the pencil lines and open flat. You should now have a large foil heart.

3. Keep heart unfolded, and place a tablespoon of mole sauce in the center of the bottom half. Place a chicken *suprème* lengthwise on top of the sauce. Top with a second tablespoon of sauce.

4. Fold the free half over and seal by overlapping the edges, beginning at the top where the heart curves and ending at the pointed end. Make as many hearts as you need.

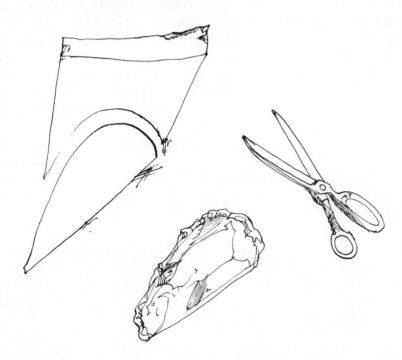

There is a more elaborate way to dress up your plate and that is with a foil "chicken," such as we saw at the famous San Angel Inn in the suburbs of Mexico City (incidentally, almost any chicken dish can be served this way). Fish was once served to us at this restaurant in these handcrafted foil chickens. (Why fish in chicken? Difficult to say.) It takes a bit of artistic skill and considerable time and patience, so we don't recommend it for large buffets, but here are the directions:

1. For each serving, tear off 32 inches of 18-inch *heavy duty* aluminum foil; place shiny side down on a work surface. Fold over 5 inches of foil at one end to give you a sturdy double thickness (Figure 1). This becomes the chicken's tail.

2. Place the foil on the table lengthwise in front of you and pleat lengthwise, accordion fashion, into ¾-inch pleats. You now have a 27-inch length of foil, ¾ of an inch wide, with a double thickness at one end (Figure 2).

3. Twist the foil once where the double thickness ends (Figure 3).

4. Keep that end (the tail end) pleated and spread the other half open. Place a small empty bottle (we use a 12-ounce Regina wine vinegar bottle) in the opened end to form the body, neck, and head of the chicken. Holding the bottle with one hand, loosely twist and compress the foil around the neck of the bottle (Figure 4). Keep it loose so that when you reach the tope of the bottle, there will be enough foil left to form the beak and the cowl of the chicken's head. A pair of pliers will aid you in this part of your work.

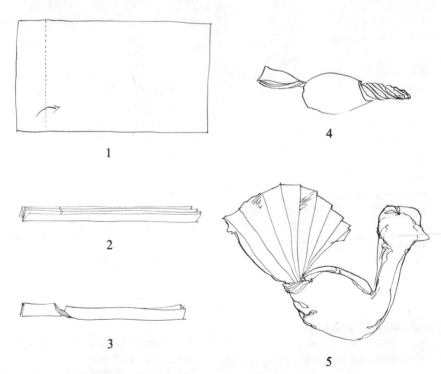

1

2

3

4

5

5. Carefully remove the bottle.

6. On the day of your party, place the mole and one cooked chicken breast inside the cavity of the foil chicken. Fold the opening over to seal. Bend each end of the chicken into an upright position to form the chicken's neck and tail.

7. Make as many chickens as you need. After they are filled and heated, the chickens' tails can be fanned handsomely outward and each bird set to rest on a "nest" of about ¾ cup of shredded red cabbage (Figure 5).

ARROZ VERDE

1½ pounds (about 4 medium) green peppers, coarsely cut
1 cup packed parsley sprigs
½ cup coarsely cut onion
1 medium clove garlic, pressed
2 teaspoons salt
⅛ teaspoon freshly ground black pepper
⅓ cup olive or vegetable oil
1½ cups long-grain white rice
2½ cups chicken broth

For 32 Servings. Three times the recipe should be sufficient.

In a food processor or blender, purée the green pepper, parsley, and onion, blending half the amount at a time. Transfer to a medium-size mixing bowl. Stir in the garlic, salt, and pepper. Heat the oil in a large skillet and sauté the rice for about 2 minutes, stirring constantly until the grains are golden. Stir in the vegetable purée and simmer for 5 minutes. Meanwhile, bring the chicken broth to a boil in a small saucepan, pour over the rice, and return to a boil. Cover the pan tightly, reduce the heat to very low, and simmer slowly for 15 to 20 minutes until the liquid is absorbed and the rice is done. Fluff with a fork and serve.

To Prepare in Advance. The rice can be prepared the day before serving, but there is no great advantage to advance preparation. To serve, sprinkle with a little water and reheat, tightly wrapped in foil, at 350° for 10 to 20 minutes (depending on quantity), or just until hot. Transfer to a warm bowl for serving.

CHILES RELLENOS DE PICADILLO

3 cans (7 ounces *each*) whole green chiles (preferably Ortega label)

1½ pounds sharp Cheddar cheese, grated

1 cup (½ pint) sour cream

⅓ cup sliced scallions

The Filling

½ cup dried currants or raisins, marinated in 2 tablespoons dry
   sherry (see *Note*)

1 pound lean ground beef

1 medium onion, minced

1 clove garlic, pressed

1½ teaspoons salt

¼ teaspoon freshly ground black pepper

⅓ cup toasted slivered almonds

⅓ cup fresh bread crumbs

For 16 Servings. Double the ingredients. Cook the filling in a large skillet, simmering about 10 minutes to reduce excess liquid. Serve in a large, shallow baking dish.

For 32 Servings. Quadruple ingredients. Cook the filling in two large skillets, simmering about 10 minutes to reduce excess liquid. Serve in two large, shallow baking dishes.

Note: We keep currants in sherry on our pantry shelf, always ready to add to a dish. Otherwise, marinate raisins no less than 6 hours before using.

Slit chiles along one side, rinse out the seeds, and dry thoroughly on paper towels. Arrange half the chiles with their sides touching in a buttered shallow 13x9-inch baking dish. Set aside.

To make the filling, heat the sherry in a saucepan with the raisins, remove from heat, and set aside to plump. In a medium-size skillet, sauté the beef with the onions and garlic about 5 minutes or until the onion is transparent. Add the salt, black pepper, almonds, and currants or raisins with their liquid. Simmer 3 to 5 minutes. Stir in the bread crumbs. Place a mound of the filling on top of the chiles in the baking dish. Cover with the remaining chiles so that each pair looks like an individually stuffed chile. Spread the cheese evenly over the top. (If you are not baking immediately, cover with plastic wrap and refrigerate.)

About 15 minutes before serving, place the cheese-covered chiles in a 350° oven. Bake, uncovered, until bubbling, about 10 to 20 minutes depending on how cold the dish was when placed in the oven. Top with dabs of sour cream and return to the oven for 3 more minutes. Garnish with sliced scallions. Serve at once.

To Prepare in Advance. Stuff the chiles and top with cheese the day before serving. Cover tightly and refrigerate. Bake just before serving, add sour cream, and return to oven for 3 more minutes.

FIESTA FRUIT BANDERILLAS
   1 bamboo skewer per serving
   Bright, shiny wrapping paper
   Double-sided Scotch tape
   5 large pieces of fruit per person (see *Note*)
   ½ large melon of your choice

Note: Choose fruit that will not darken on standing, such as strawberries, chunks of cantaloupe, honeydew, watermelon, or pineapple. Jícama, a crispy white tuber, is an authentic and novel addition. Avoid small fruits or melon balls—too ordinary. If you use bananas or apples, dip them in lemon juice, or treat them with Fruit Fresh, following package directions. Fruit Fresh, a powdered ascorbic acid (vitamin C), available at most markets, will keep fruit from darkening without affecting the flavor.

To make paper frills for the ends of the skewers, cut wrapping paper into 5x2-inch rectangles. Fold each rectangle in half lengthwise, colored side in if only one side has color. Fold in quarters. Along the folded edge, cut down about three quarters of the way, repeating every ⅛ inch to form a fringelike paper eyelash (Figure 1). Unfold. Turn colored side out. Place double-sided Scotch tape along one raw edge, allowing a 1-inch excess of tape at each end. Fold the tape over to seal the raw edge. Use the end of the tape to attach the frill to an area 2 inches from the end of a skewer and wrap the paper around the skewer, working toward the point of the skewer. The tape will stick to itself and to the skewer (Figure 2). Once attached, twirl the skewer in your hand to open the frills (these are easier to make than they sound).

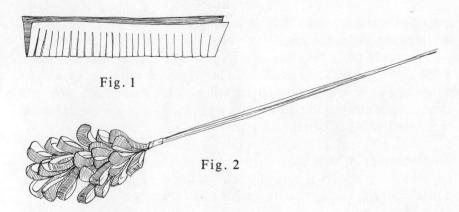

Fig. 1

Fig. 2

Spear 5 chunks of cut fruit on each skewer. To serve, spear the skewers into half a melon placed cut side down on a plate, or arrange like spokes on a wheel on a large round serving plate.

To Prepare in Advance. The fruit can be skewered up to 4 hours before serving. Cover (fruit only, not frills) with a damp towel and keep chilled until ready to serve.

MANGO SHERBET
For 16 small servings

> 3 or 4 large ripe mangoes
> ¾ cup sugar
> ⅔ cup freshly squeezed, strained orange juice
> ⅓ cup freshly squeezed, strained lemon juice
> ⅓ cup freshly squeezed, strained lime juice
> ½ cup light corn syrup (Karo)
> 2 cups milk

The Garnish
> 16 thin slices of lime (2 limes)
> 16 small nontoxic flowers (such as bougainvillaea or daisies)

Cut each mango parallel to the flat seed and remove the seed. Blend all the pulp in a food processor or blender until smooth. Measure 1½ cups of the purée into a small heavy saucepan. Stir in the sugar and place the pan over low heat. Simmer for about 3 minutes until the sugar has dissolved. Remove from heat and stir in the remaining ingredients. (Don't worry if the milk appears curdled. It will clear upon freezing.) Pour into ice trays or other freezer containers. Freeze.

To make individual servings, soften the sherbet slightly at room temperature and scoop small servings into individual ramekins or miniature soufflé dishes. Return to the freezer. When ready to serve, place the ramekins on a tray or large basket, garnish each with a slice of lime pierced through the center with a flower, and serve.

To Prepare in Advance. If tightly covered, the sherbet keeps in the freezer up to three weeks. For convenience, spoon into serving dishes the day before the party. Prepare the lime slices and flower garnish several hours before serving. Cover with damp towels until ready to use.

ICED MARGARITA SOUFFLÉ

¼ cup Cointreau or Triple Sec
2 tablespoons cold water
1½ tablespoons (1½ envelopes) unflavored gelatin
6 egg yolks
¾ cup sugar
1 cup milk, heated
¾ cup freshly squeezed, strained lime juice (about 7 limes)
Zest (green peel) of 1 large lime, finely chopped
10 egg whites, at room temperature
¼ teaspoon salt
¼ teaspoon cream of tartar, or 1 teaspoon fresh lemon juice
1½ cups heavy cream (whipping cream)
5 drops green food coloring

The Garnish

½ cup heavy cream, whipped and sweetened with 1 tablespoon
  sifted powdered sugar
10 or more candied violets, or other colorful, nontoxic fresh flowers

For 16 Servings. Make the recipe twice. Mold in two soufflé dishes or mound in a large bowl and call it Margarita Mousse.

For 32 Servings. Some guests will eat little or no dessert. Make one single and one double recipe. Mold the single recipe in a soufflé dish and mound the rest in a large serving bowl.

To form the soufflé collar, tear off a length of aluminum foil or wax paper long enough to wrap around a 6-cup (1½-quart) soufflé dish.Fold it in half lengthwise and oil the inside lightly. Wrap it around the dish and secure with a string just below the rim of the dish to form a collar that will stand 3 inches above the rim of the dish.

To make the filling, combine the Cointreau or Triple Sec and water in a small bowl. Sprinkle the gelatin over the top and set aside to soften for 5 minutes. Meanwhile, in the top of a double boiler, beat the egg yolks and sugar until light and lemon colored. Stir in the hot milk and the softened gelatin. Cook over hot water for about 5 minutes, stirring constantly until the custard coats the spoon. Remove from heat and transfer to a large mixing bowl. Stir in the lime juice and zest; refrigerate until the mixture begins to set, stirring from time to time until syrupy.

In a large bowl, beat the egg whites with the salt and the cream of tartar or lemon juice until the whites do not slide when the bowl is tilted. Set aside. Blend the cream until it holds its shape. Whip in the food coloring. Fold the whipped cream into the lime mixture. Fold in half the egg whites thoroughly; carefully fold in the remaining half. When well combined, pour into the prepared dish. Swirl the top of the mixture decoratively and chill for at least 4 hours.

Before serving, whip the cream and sweeten with the powdered sugar pressed through a sieve with the back of a spoon. Decorate the top of the soufflé with puffs or rosettes of whipped cream topped with candied violets. To serve, spoon the soufflé onto dessert plates or into stemmed glasses.

To Prepare in Advance. The soufflé will keep for two days in the refrigerator or for two weeks in the freezer. If frozen, thaw overnight in the refrigerator before serving. The whipped cream for the decoration can be prepared and kept chilled in the refrigerator 4 hours before serving.

ENCORES

With the extra food you can have a family fiesta within a day or two. The punch, though diluted, will keep for days in the refrigerator. Freshen it by adding the leftover skewered fruit, fresh juices, or any of the punch ingredients. The peanuts will keep for a long time and are great as a snack. The guacamole will have darkened and cannot be restored. The Chicken Mole and Arroz Verde can be heated separately in sealed foil packages for 15 minutes in a 350° oven, along with the Chiles Rellenos, which should be heated uncovered. Serve with frozen Mango Sherbet. Spoon portions of leftover Margarita Soufflé into champagne glasses and refrigerate to serve within 24 hours.

FIVE-SAUCE SPAGHETTI FEAST

Menu

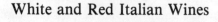

White and Red Italian Wines

Antipasto Platter

Large Bowl of Steaming Homemade Pasta

Sauces
Italian Sausage-Flavored Sauce
Sauce Bolognese
Pesto Genovese
Red Clam Sauce
White Clam Sauce

Condiments
Freshly Grated Parmesan
Freshly Chopped Herbs
Dried Chili Flakes

Toasted Garlic Rolls

Basket of Fresh Seasonal Fruit and

Tray of Italian Cheeses or

Ricotta Cheese Pie in a Macaroon Crust

Espresso

FIVE-SAUCE SPAGHETTI FEAST

We make our own pasta using a pasta machine and freeze extra amounts for more Five-Sauce Spaghetti Feasts. And feast it is. The antipasto whets guests' appetites for the pasta—spaghetti, served with a choice of five boldly flavored sauces.

Our recipe for Homemade Pasta requires the use of a pasta machine; it is best to buy pasta if you don't have a machine. The Italian Sausage-Flavored Sauce makes an ideal spaghetti sauce. The ingredients listed in the Sauce Bolognese may sound odd, but the sauce is unbelievably popular with our guests. Fresh clams are steamed right in the Red Clam Sauce, and from the Royal Danieli in Venice, Italy, we learned to stir in fresh butter, just before serving. The White Clam Sauce is not white; it is simply not red. The tomatoes used do not color the sauce red—they just add specks of red here and there. Some restaurants use a cream sauce base, which is not authentically Italian. The Pesto Genovese, redolent with its fresh sweet basil, is delicious.

Cooking the spaghetti is the only last-minute main chore you have; cook it in small batches: It is at its best directly out of the pot, you can judge the amounts needed if additional guests show up or some fail to arrive, and you will not have mounds of spaghetti left over. Though it keeps well, spaghetti loses much of its character if refrigerated. Leftover sauces, on the other hand, mellow with age.

A plate of spaghetti with Toasted Garlic Rolls makes a substantial meal, so we prefer something light for dessert. Italian cheeses and artfully designed fruit baskets complement each other well. For a more sophisticated dessert, serve the Ricotta Cheese Pie, which appears in the Lavish Italian Summertime Buffet. Espresso, served black, is traditionally served after dinner in Italy.

THE TABLE SETTINGS

This is a casual, single-line, seated buffet. Fork (or fork and spoon) only is required; silverware and napkins are at preset tables. Wines, appetizers, and desserts are served separately.

Centerpieces

Buffet Table. You will need a shallow, rectangular basket; a round of Provolone cheese encased in wax and tied with twine (available in Italian markets); a 6-inch stick of Italian salami; ½ pound long, thin spaghetti; a long loaf of Italian bread; and an assortment of the following: red-leaf lettuce, red onions, red bell peppers, green bell peppers, eggplant, red cabbage, whole heads of garlic. Arrange these items in the basket to create a dramatic Mediterranean centerpiece, keeping the colors of the Italian flag (red, white, and green) dominant. Keep the spaghetti loose so that it fans out at one end of the basket. Tuck in the bread (which can be a day old and varnished, if you wish) to overhang the other end. This centerpiece can be assembled the day before the

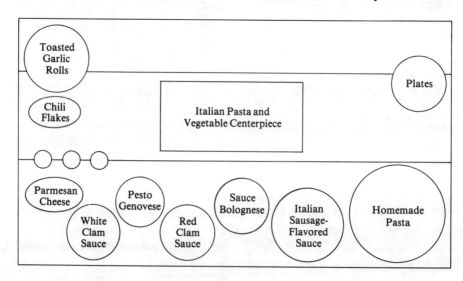

party, except for the lettuce and salami, which should be added just before guests arrive.

Dining Tables. For each centerpiece, you will need a flowerpot filled with bunches of parsley and fresh flowers. As part of the decor, place salt and pepper in tiny flowerpot saucers.

Artichoke Candles. To make each candle, you will need one artichoke, pliers, and a votive candle with a glass holder. Cut off the stem of the artichoke flush with the base so that the artichoke stands upright. Remove the center leaves with the pliers and place the candle in the hollow. Artichoke candles can be used as table decorations or placed in an arrangement of raw vegetables. Prepare the day before (wrap in damp paper towels and refrigerate) or the morning of your party. Light the candles just before guests arrive.

TIMETABLE

This party, which has an abundance of sauces, requires planning but very little last-minute bother. All the sauces, except the White Clam Sauce, can be made days or even weeks ahead and frozen. If you plan to make homemade pasta, do it at your convenience and dry or freeze it.

Three Days Before the Party. If you are planning to serve the Ricotta Cheese Pie, make it and store it in the refrigerator.

The Day Before the Party. Buy the fresh clams for the Red Clam Sauce and store them on ice or in an open bag in the bottom part of the

refrigerator. Heat the garlic in butter for garlic bread. Make the White
Clam Sauce. Cool, add reserved clams, and chill. Thaw pesto if frozen.
Chill the white wine. If artichoke candles are to be part of your decora-
tion, prepare them now, wrap in damp paper towels, and refrigerate.

The Day of the Party. Arrange the antipasto tray, cover with damp
paper towels, and refrigerate. In the afternoon, grate fresh Parmesan,
add some to the pesto, and place the rest in a serving bowl on the table,
covered with foil to retain freshness. Chop fresh herbs, such as basil
and oregano, and store separately, covered with plastic wrap, in the
refrigerator. Scrub and soak the fresh clams. Butter the garlic bread,
ready for last-minute broiling. If you are serving the fruit and cheese
dessert, arrange the cheeses on a tray, completely covering the surface
of each cheese with plastic wrap. Set in a cool place, but do not refrigerate. Arrange the basket of fresh fruits next to the cheese tray, along
with crackers and plates for self-service.

COUNTDOWN

45 minutes before guests arrive:	Bring antipasto to room temperature.
	Open red wines "to breathe" and place in cool place with open bottles of white wine on ice for self-service.
	Place sauces in pots for reheating.
	Put herbs and chiles on buffet table.
	In low oven warm bowls for serving of pasta and sauces.
Just before guests arrive:	Bring covered pots of water to a boil for the pasta.
	Bring pie to room temperature.
	Remove paper towels and plastic wrap from antipasto, herbs, and cheese.
	Prepare coffee and boil water for tea.
20 minutes before serving:	Slowly heat all sauces, except white clam sauce and pesto.
	Put fresh clams in red sauce, and simmer, covered, 10 to 15 minutes.
	Preheat broiler.
	Finish pesto.

5 to 10 minutes before serving:	Cook pasta, just until *al dente*.
	Drain and put in warm bowl.
	Finish all the sauces and set them out with the pasta.
5 minutes before serving:	Broil garlic bread and place in serving basket.
	Announce dinner.

RECIPES

ANTIPASTO PLATTER

1 basket cherry tomatoes, or 8 ounces cherry peppers, drained
1 bunch parsley
8 ounces salami, cubed
8 ounces mortadella, cubed
8 ounces marinated mushrooms
8 ounces Provolone cheese, cubed
4 ounces marinated artichoke hearts
4 ounces smoked oysters or clams
Pickled Italian peppers
Carrot sticks
Radishes, decoratively cut

Mound the cherry tomatoes or cherry peppers in the center of a large serving plate. Wreath with a row of parsley clusters. Arrange the remaining ingredients around the outside, spoke-fashion. Insert cocktail picks. Serve at room temperature.

To Prepare in Advance. The platter can be arranged the morning of your party. Cover with a damp paper towel and refrigerate. Bring to room temperature about 1 hour before serving. Remove towel and serve.

HOMEMADE PASTA
For 1½ pounds, or 8 servings

> 3 cups unbleached all-purpose flour
> 3 large eggs
> 1 tablespoon olive oil
> 1 teaspoon salt
> 2 or more tablespoons lukewarm water (or puréed cooked spinach for green noodles)

For 32 Servings. Make two double batches for ease in handling.

Place the flour in a large mixing bowl and make a well in the center; drop in the eggs, olive oil, and salt. Mix together with your fingers or a fork until crumbly. Sprinkle in the warm water (or spinach purée) 1 tablespoon at a time, while you mix, press, and knead the dough against the sides and bottom of the bowl until it can be gathered into a ball. Add more water only if you cannot work dough into a ball. The dough should not be sticky. If it is, you have added too much water: Work in a little more flour until the dough is no longer sticky.

Divide the dough into four balls and place each one in a plastic bag or under plastic wrap to prevent drying out while you work.

To make the pasta in a pasta machine, place the gauge of the rollers as far apart as possible at the widest notch. Flatten one piece of dough with your palm, flour it lightly into a ¼- to ⅓-inch thick rectangle. Feed the rectangle through the rollers of the machine. It will emerge as a ragged sheet. Fold the sheet in half, crosswise, flour slightly, and run it through the rollers again. Repeat this folding, flouring, and rolling process about 8 times, until the dough is very smooth, shiny, and elastic. The machine does all the kneading for you. Lightly flour the sheet of dough and lay it on a strip of waxed paper or kitchen towel to rest while you work the remaining portions of dough.

When all the sheets are rolled, set the machine two notches closer and feed the first piece of dough through the rollers again. Reroll the dough 4 or 5 more times, folding, dusting lightly with flour if sticky, moving the rollers closer with each rolling, and putting it through the machine until the sheet is the proper thickness—about 1/16 inch. Machines vary, so you might have to experiment a bit.

Let the sheets of pasta dry 10 minutes before running through the cutting rollers. For spaghetti or tagliarini, the pasta should be ⅛-inch wide; for fettuccine, ½-inch wide; or for lasagna noodles, use squares the width of the machine rollers. As you cut the noodles, place them on a well-floured towel, shaking the noodles so that they will not stick together and coating them lightly but thoroughly with the flour. Pasta should dry at least 30 minutes before it is cooked or covered tightly with plastic wrap and kept in the refrigerator as long as 24 hours.

To Prepare in Advance. Homemade pasta may be made weeks ahead and frozen. (It can also be dried, which we don't recommend.) Let rest about 2 hours at room temperature, then flour lightly and arrange loosely in storage containers (we use foil pie tins) and seal in plastic bags. Lasagna squares should be well floured before stacking and wrapping. It is not necessary to thaw pasta before dropping into boiling water.

HOW TO COOK PASTA

For each pound of pasta, use at least 6 quarts of boiling water, 2 tablespoons of salt, and 1 tablespoon of oil. When the water is boiling rapidly, add the pasta slowly so that the boiling temperature is maintained throughout the cooking until the pasta is done. Test the pasta often for doneness. The time it takes to cook will vary according to the thickness of the pasta and whether it is fresh or dried. It should always be cooked *al dente,* literally "to the tooth," or firm (1 to 2 minutes if fresh, 5 to 10 minutes if dried). When done, drain immediately into a colander. It is not necessary to rinse pasta if you have used sufficient water, but if you prefer you can rinse it with boiling water or very hot tap water. Drain well. Place in a hot serving bowl, toss lightly with butter, and salt, if the pasta has been rinsed. Serve immediately with a wooden spaghetti lifter.

To Prepare in Advance. We have tried every conceivable way to cook pasta in advance. We even tried undercooking it considerably, but in vain. There is no way to keep pasta firm and fresh tasting until served. Leftover spaghetti can, of course, be reheated, but it won't taste as good.

ITALIAN SAUSAGE-FLAVORED SAUCE

For 6 cups, or 8 servings (or up to 32 servings if all the sauces are served)

1½ pounds sweet or hot Italian sausage (or a combination of both)
1 large onion, chopped
2 medium cloves garlic, pressed
1 (1-pound 12-ounce) can Italian-style tomatoes
2 (6 ounces *each*) cans tomato paste
1¼ cups dry white wine, or 1 cup dry vermouth
¼ cup chopped parsley
1 tablespoon salt
1 tablespoon sugar (if using hot Italian sausage)
¼ teaspoon freshly ground black pepper (if using sweet Italian sausage)
¼ cup sweet basil, chopped, or 1 tablespoon dried sweet basil, crumbled
1 teaspoon Worcestershire sauce

Remove the sausage meat from the casings and place it in a 5- or 6-quart skillet over medium heat. Crumble the sausage; add the onion and garlic and cook about 15 minutes, breaking up the sausage with the back of a wooden spoon until it is browned and crumbly and the onion and garlic are cooked. Stir in the remaining sauce ingredients, bring to a simmer; cook, uncovered, over very low heat for about 1½ hours, or until thick. Stir the sauce often toward the end of the cooking time to prevent scorching. Remove from heat and skim and discard the fat from the top.

To Prepare in Advance. This sauce improves in flavor if made at least one day before serving. Reheat gently in a heavy saucepan. It will keep up to five days in the refrigerator. It freezes well and may be made three months in advance.

SAUCE BOLOGNESE

For 6 cups, or 8 servings (or up to 32 servings if all the sauces are served)

¼ pound lean bacon, finely diced
1 tablespoon olive oil
3 medium onions, minced
3 medium carrots, finely diced
3 stalks celery, finely diced

4 medium cloves garlic, minced or pressed
1½ pounds lean ground beef
6 chicken livers, minced
1 (6-ounce) can tomato paste
3 cups dry white wine, or 1½ cups dry vermouth
½ cup minced parsley
1½ teaspoons beef extract (see *Note*)
1 tablespoon Italian herb seasoning, or ½ teaspoon *each* dried ore-
    gano, marjoram, thyme, and sweet basil
2 bay leaves
1 long strip lemon zest (yellow peel)
½ teaspoon freshly ground black pepper
Salt
¾ cup heavy cream (whipping cream)

To Serve

Freshly grated Parmesan cheese

Note: Beef extract can be purchased at specialty food stores. Or it can
be made by reducing beef stock or brown sauce until thick. If stored in
the refrigerator, it will keep indefinitely. In a pinch, substitute 1 beef
bouillon cube for each ½ teaspoon called for in a recipe.

In a large, heavy, medium-size enameled or stainless-steel skillet
(not iron, which will discolor any mixture containing tomatoes or wine),
sauté the diced bacon over medium heat until most of the fat is rendered. Remove the bacon from the pan and set aside. Add the olive oil
and onions to the bacon drippings in the skillet. Sauté the onions about
5 minutes until they are transparent. Add the carrots, celery, and garlic.
Cook over medium-high heat, stirring often, until the vegetables are
lightly browned. Add the ground beef and the reserved bacon to the
pan, breaking up the beef with the back of a spoon until cooked and
crumbly. Stir in the chicken livers and cook briefly. Add all the remaining ingredients, except the cream. Simmer about 45 minutes, or until the
sauce is quite thick. Before serving, stir in the cream, heat through, and
serve over hot cooked pasta with freshly grated Parmesan.

To Prepare in Advance. This sauce improves in flavor if made at least
one day before serving to the point *before* the cream is added. It will
keep up to four days in the refrigerator. Reheat gently in a heavy
saucepan, add the cream, and the Parmesan cheese when serving. It
freezes well and can be made three months in advance.

PESTO GENOVESE

For 2 cups, or 8 servings (or up to 32 servings if all the sauces are served)

>2 cups fresh sweet basil, stemmed (see *Note 1*)
>½ cup parsley flowers, packed
>½ cup olive oil
>¼ cup chopped walnuts (see *Note 2*)
>2 medium cloves garlic
>1 ¼ teaspoons salt
>¾ cup freshly grated Parmesan cheese
>4 tablespoons (½ stick) butter, at room temperature

For 16 Servings. A double recipe can be made in a blender or food processor in one batch.

For 32 Servings. Two double recipes should be sufficient unless you are serving other sauces.

Note 1: Fresh sweet basil is an easy herb to grow. Each spring we set out small plants in clay pots on our kitchen patio and snip leaves away all summer to use in various dishes. At the end of the growing season, we snip the remaining leaves and make this pesto for the freezer. To measure, gently pack the basil leaves into a measuring cup.

Note 2: Pine nuts *(pignoli)* are the traditional ingredient, but they are expensive and sometimes hard to obtain; we have discovered that walnuts make a very good substitute.

Combine the basil, parsley, olive oil, walnuts, garlic, and salt in the container of a blender or food processor. Process at high speed, stopping the motor occasionally to scrape down the sides of the container with a rubber spatula. When well blended, add the Parmesan cheese; blend only a second or two to mix. Add the butter; blend only a second or two. Do not overblend or you will lose the texture of the cheese. Serve the pesto at room temperature. If serving with pasta, thin with about a tablespoon of the boiling water in which the pasta was cooked.

To Prepare in Advance. Pesto freezes well. Combine all the ingredients, except the Parmesan cheese and butter, and freeze in a capped jar. To thaw, set the jar in warm water, then mix in the Parmesan and butter as described above. Leftover pesto can be frozen up to three months ahead with the cheese and butter added, but the cheese will lose some of its fresh flavor. If not frozen, it will keep at least a week in the refrigerator.

RED CLAM SAUCE
For 6 cups, or 8 servings (or up to 32 servings if all the sauces are served)

> 1 medium onion, minced
> 2 cloves garlic, pressed
> 2 tablespoons olive oil
> 2 pounds fresh ripe tomatoes, peeled, or 1 (1-pound 12-ounce) can Italian-style tomatoes with juice
> 1 (6-ounce) can tomato paste
> 2 cups homemade fish stock or bottled clam juice
> ¾ cup dry white wine or ⅔ cup dry vermouth
> 1 tablespoon fresh sweet basil, chopped, or 1 teaspoon dried sweet basil, crumbled
> ½ teaspoon dried oregano, crumbled
> 1 teaspoon sugar
> 1 teaspoon salt
> Pinch dried red pepper flakes, or several dashes cayenne
> 32 clams in the shell (see Note)
> 3 tablespoons butter
> ¼ cup minced parsley

For 16 to 32 Servings. The recipe may be doubled. Simmer 1½ hours or until the sauce has thickened to the desired consistency.

Note: Fresh live clams have a dull, not hollow, sound when they are clicked together. Buy them at a reputable fish market within 24 hours of cooking. If you do not plan to use them immediately, store them in an *open* bag in the bottom part of the refrigerator or on ice. Up to three hours before cooking, rinse the clams well to remove any outside sand. Place them in a large pot or bowl with cold water to cover. Add a handful of salt to the water. Soaking the clams in this manner gets rid of any sand that still remains inside. Then drain and wash well to remove all sand.

In a heavy, medium-size enameled or stainless-steel skillet (do not use iron, which will discolor any mixture containing tomatoes or wine), sauté the onion and garlic in the olive oil about 5 minutes until the onion is transparent. Stir in the tomatoes, breaking them up against the sides of the pan with the edge of a wooden spoon. Add the tomato paste, clam juice, wine, sweet basil, oregano, sugar, salt, and red pepper. Simmer slowly, uncovered, for 30 to 40 minutes until the sauce has thickened to the desired consistency. Taste and correct the seasoning.

About 20 minutes before serving, combine the presoaked clams and the sauce in a large kettle or Dutch oven with a tight-fitting lid. Simmer over low heat for 10 to 15 minutes until all the clams have opened. Discard any that have not opened. Remove the pan from the heat and with a slotted spoon transfer the clams to a warm serving bowl. Stir the butter and half the parsley into the sauce. Pour the sauce over the clams and sprinkle the remaining parsley over the sauce.

To Prepare in Advance. Like most sauces, Red Clam Sauce will improve in flavor if it is made (up to the point before the clams are added) at least one day before serving. Store in the refrigerator up to four days or in the freezer up to three months. Just before serving, add the fresh clams and finish the sauce according to the above directions.

WHITE CLAM SAUCE
About 1 quart, or 8 servings (up to 32 servings if all the sauces are served)

>   3 large cloves garlic, cut in halves
>   ⅓ cup olive oil
>   ½ cup minced shallots
>   1 (8-ounce) bottle clam juice
>   2 (10 ounces *each*) cans whole baby clams with juice
>   3 cups dry white wine
>   2 large tomatoes, peeled, seeded, and diced
>   2 tablespoons chopped fresh oregano, or 2 teaspoons dried oregano, crumbled
>   ½ to ¾ teaspoon freshly ground black pepper
>   ½ cup minced parsley

For 32 Servings. Make two recipes in separate pans. Do not double recipe.

In a heavy, medium-size enameled or stainless-steel skillet (do not use iron, which will discolor any mixture containing tomatoes or wine), sauté the cut garlic in the olive oil until golden. Stir in the shallots (do not let them brown), followed by the clam juice, the juice from the canned baby clams (reserve the clams), the wine, tomatoes, oregano, and pepper. Cook over medium heat, covered, for 5 minutes. Remove the cover and reduce the sauce over high heat for 15 to 20 minutes. Remove garlic cloves. Stir in the parsley and reserved clams. Heat just until clams are heated through. Serve in a warm bowl to be spooned over hot cooked pasta.

To Prepare in Advance. If making the sauce a day ahead, let it cool, add the clams, and refrigerate. When ready to serve, stir in the chopped parsley and reheat the sauce gently. Do not freeze.

CONDIMENTS FOR SPAGHETTI

Parmesan Cheese. Freshly grated, this is a must. Be sure to buy the imported *Parmigiano-Reggiano.* Allow about 1 ounce per person. It is easily "grated" when cut into ½-inch cubes in a food processor fitted with the steel blade, not the shredder, or in an electric blender.

Fresh Herbs. Especially appropriate are sweet basil, oregano, and Italian-style flat leaf parsley. People won't use much, so about ½ cup of each, chopped, should be sufficient for 16 servings; ¾ cup for 32 servings.

Chile Flakes. These are available dried. A very small bowl or ½ cup will serve 32.

TOASTED GARLIC ROLLS

¼ pound (1 stick) butter or margarine
1 to 2 cloves garlic, pressed
1 tablespoon minced parsley
4 French rolls
¼ cup grated Parmesan cheese (optional)
Paprika

In a small saucepan or skillet, melt the butter with the garlic. Simmer very slowly for 5 minutes, remove from heat, and let stand for no less than 1 hour. Stir in the parsley.

Preheat the oven to 400°. Slice the rolls in half lengthwise. Dip the cut side in the garlic butter and place buttered side up on a baking sheet that will fit under the broiler. Sprinkle with Parmesan cheese, if desired, and a few sprinklings of paprika for color. Bake in the oven for 10 minutes, then slide the baking sheet under the broiler for a few seconds to crisp and brown the top. Serve hot.

To Prepare in Advance. The garlic butter can be made the day before, and the rolls prepared for baking at least 6 hours ahead. Cover loosely and leave at room temperature. Bake and brown just before serving.

BASKET OF FRESH SEASONAL FRUIT

In a basket, arrange an assortment of grapes, plums, pears, apricots, and apples.

TRAY OF ITALIAN CHEESES

Allow about 2 ounces per person of the following assortment: Taleggio, Gorgonzola, and Bel Paese. Arrange attractively on a cheese board.

ESPRESSO

A good "instant" powdered espresso is made by the Spice Islands Company for those who do not have an espresso machine. Follow directions on the bottle. Serve black, in very small portions.

ENCORES

Leftover cooked spaghetti can be stored in the refrigerator and reheated. It won't remain *al dente,* but it will still be delicious family fare with any leftover sauces. If all the sauces are made, you will definitely have leftovers. If sauces have not been previously frozen, they can be frozen for future use, except for the White Clam Sauce, which does not freeze well. Remaining antipasto items will keep several days in the refrigerator. The vegetables in the centerpiece make a crunchy salad or an imaginative soup or stew into which you can toss some of the fresh herbs. Trim and wrap the cheeses airtight in plastic wrap. Refrigerate. Serve them the next day with the bread from the centerpiece (if you didn't varnish it). Freeze the grated Parmesan. It need not be thawed before using.

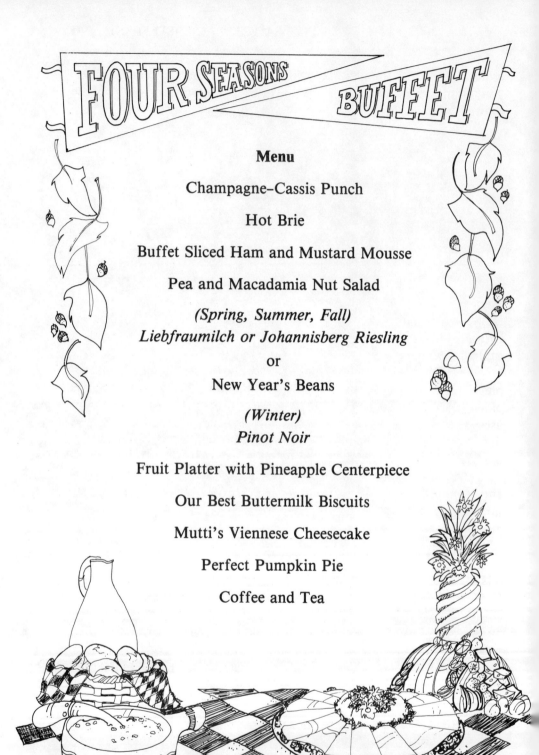

FOUR SEASONS BUFFET

Menu

Champagne–Cassis Punch

Hot Brie

Buffet Sliced Ham and Mustard Mousse

Pea and Macadamia Nut Salad

(Spring, Summer, Fall)
Liebfraumilch or Johannisberg Riesling

or

New Year's Beans

(Winter)
Pinot Noir

Fruit Platter with Pineapple Centerpiece

Our Best Buttermilk Biscuits

Mutti's Viennese Cheesecake

Perfect Pumpkin Pie

Coffee and Tea

THE FOUR SEASONS BUFFET

This buffet is suitable for any afternoon or early evening and for any occasion—from a garden wedding to a New Year's Day gathering to watch the football game. It is also ideal for one- or two-line buffets and for very large gatherings. Once the food is in place, supplies are easily replenished from the kitchen.

The punch and appetizer are easy to prepare. The oversized fruit platter is eye-catching with its tropical flower-studded, spiral-cut pineapple and its array of colorful in-season fruits. If dining tables are used, place the butter and honey for the biscuits on them rather than on the buffet table to avoid holding up the buffet line. Second-serving baskets of hot biscuits can be brought to the tables by a helper.

The ham is wreathed around a brilliant yellow Mustard Mousse and is suitable either hot for a hearty dinner or cold for a luncheon or sandwich-making supper. For holiday buffets, you might use a ring mold with a wreath pattern for the mousse.

The unusual crisp Pea and Macadamia Nut Salad is a specialty of our good friend, Mildred Mead. The alternative recipe for winter buffets is New Year's Beans. The recipe comes to us via our friend, Barbara Garrett, from her friend, Martha Brown, who calls them Fourth of July Beans. We substituted black-eyed peas for the limas and changed the name to fit an old Southern superstition: Eating black-eyed peas on New Year's Day brings good luck.

And to crown this Four Seasons Buffet, we offer two desserts: a cloudlike cheesecake with a rose garnish and a Perfect Pumpkin Pie recipe from our friend, Jerry Jerabek, who shared this recipe with us ten years ago. Since then we've made some minor changes, but it still remains our favorite holiday pie.

The recipe for the Champagne-Cassis Punch appears in the Exotic Curry and Chutney Buffet, and the Hot Brie can be found in the Elegant Open House Buffet.

THE TABLE SETTINGS

This a single- or double-line seated buffet. Knife and fork are required; silverware and napkins are at preset tables, unless you are planning a lap buffet, in which case place them on the buffet table as illustrated. Beverages, appetizer, and desserts are served separately.

Centerpieces.

The Buffet Table. Fruit platter with pineapple centerpiece. See the Recipes section of this buffet for directions on how to assemble.

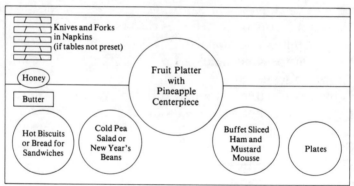

Setup for a single-line buffet.

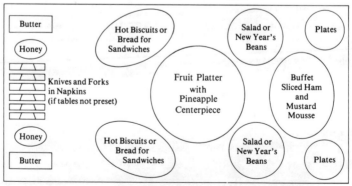

Setup for a double-line buffet.

The Dining Tables. For each centerpiece, you will need a round basket, a head of red-leaf lettuce, and cherry tomatoes. Cut off about 1 inch from the stem end of the lettuce. Fluff the leaves slightly and stand the head in the basket. Spray with nonstick cooking spray to give the leaves a sheen and arrange the tomatoes on the folds. Spray with a mister to keep fresh and moist. The centerpieces can be assembled and misted 6 hours before the party.

TIMETABLE

Three Days Before the Party. If you are serving New Year's Beans, bake the beans. The recipe is generous. If it is more than your guests can eat, serve ahead of time to friends or family. It can also be frozen up to three months in advance. Toast the almonds for the Hot Brie. Make the cheesecake.

Up to Two Days Before the Party. Make the Mustard Mousse.

The Day Before the Party. Make the pea salad, if serving, carve the pineapple for the fruit platter, and marinate the currants or raisins for the cheesecake. Slice the ham, or have a delicatessen do it for you. Store slices stacked together to prevent drying. Soften the butter to be served with the biscuits, transfer it to serving crocks, and keep chilled. Make the ice ring for the punch. Make the pie if you cannot make it the day of the party.

The Morning of the Party. Set out the dry ingredients and the baking pan for the biscuits. If you haven't already made the pumpkin pie, make it now. Assemble the centerpieces up to 6 hours before the party. Within 6 hours of serving, unmold the Mustard Mousse and keep it chilled. Within 4 hours of serving, arrange the fruit on a platter if you have enough refrigerator storage space and the fruit will not darken; otherwise, complete the platter just before guests arrive. Spoon the pea salad onto lettuce leaves on a serving platter and keep chilled. Place the Brie topped with almonds in its baking dish in the refrigerator. Decorate the Viennese cheesecake and leave at room temperature. Whip the cream for the pumpkin pie and store in the serving bowl in the refrigerator. Chill the champagne for the punch.

COUNTDOWN

1 hour before guest arrive:	Mix and bake the biscuits if they are to be reheated for serving.

	Arrange parsley and pineapple, cover with damp paper towels, and place on table(s).
	Arrange ham with parsley on platter, leaving room for the Mustard Mousse. Cover with damp paper towels.
30 minutes before guests arrive:	Reheat beans in crock pot or slow-oven (250°).
15 minutes before guests arrive:	Prepare coffee and tea.
	Unmold ice ring and place in punch bowl.
10 minutes before guests arrive:	Put out all food, except mousse, hot beans, and biscuits.
Just before guests arrive:	Combine punch ingredients in punch bowl.
	Remove towels from food.
	Add rest of fruit and flowers to pineapple platter.
As guests arrive:	Heat Brie at 475° until soft. Serve with crackers.
15 minutes before serving:	Mix and bake biscuits if they are to be served fresh.
	Place mousse in center of ham platter.
	Set out hot beans.
	Announce the meal.
	(Before serving pumpkin pie, heat for 7 to 10 minutes at 300°.)

RECIPES

BUFFET SLICED HAM

For 16 servings

    3 pounds lean, boneless, fully cooked ham (preferably "Black Forest" or "Honey Baked" variety)

    1 bunch parsley, stemmed

Slice the ham yourself or have it sliced at a delicatessen into even ⅛-inch-thick slices. Arrange the slices in wavelike rolls around a large circular platter to encircle the mustard mousse. Insert a parsley sprig in the end of each roll. (Any other serving platter practical for your buffet can be used.)

To Prepare in Advance. Slice the ham the day before serving. Stack it neatly together to prevent drying out and tightly wrap in plastic wrap. Within 1 hours of serving, arrange the ham on the platter, insert parsley, and cover with a damp towel until serving time.

MUSTARD MOUSSE
For 16 servings

½ cup sugar
2 tablespoons dry mustard (preferably Coleman's label)
1 tablespoon (1 envelope) plain gelatin
¾ teaspoon ground turmeric
1 teaspoon celery salt
4 large eggs, at room temperature
1 cup water
½ cup white wine vinegar or cider vinegar
1 cup heavy cream (whipping cream)

The Garnish
1 bunch parsley, stemmed
5 to 7 fresh flowers

Prepare a 5- or 6-cup ring mold according to directions under Molds in the Garnishes appendix.

You can make the base of the mousse quickly if you use a heavy-bottomed, nonaluminum saucepan or skillet instead of a double boiler and stir the mixture constantly over low heat.

In a saucepan or skillet combine the sugar, mustard, gelatin, turmeric, and celery salt. Stir to break up the mustard lumps. Beat in the eggs with a whisk until thoroughly combined, then add the water and vinegar. Place the pan over low heat and whisk the mixture constantly until the gelatin dissolves and the mixture thickens slightly, taking care not to curdle the mixture with too much heat. Transfer to a mixing bowl and chill (in the refrigerator or over ice cubes) until the mixture mounds slightly when dropped from a spoon. If you chill until firm, reliquify over warm water.

Whip the cream until it holds a soft shape; do not overbeat. Fold it into the mustard mixture and turn the mousse into the prepared mold. Chill several hours until set.

To unmold the mousse, we find it practical to turn it out onto a plate just large enough to hold it and refrigerate until serving time. Then place the mousse (with the plate) in the center of the large ham platter and surround it with the ham rolls as described in the preceding recipe. You can also unmold the mousse directly onto a large round platter and refrigerate it if you have space.

Stem the parsley and cluster it in the center of the mousse. Tuck in the fresh flowers. Provide a serving fork for the ham and a silver slicer for the mousse.

To Prepare in Advance. The mousse can be made up to two days ahead and refrigerated in the mold. Unmold up to 6 hours ahead and keep chilled.

PEA AND MACADAMIA NUT SALAD

1 (10-ounce) package frozen "petite" peas
1 cup diced celery
1 cup chopped macadamia nuts (or cashews)
¼ cup thinly sliced scallions, including part of the green stems
¼ cup Crisp Bacon Bits (see Recipes index)

The Dressing

¼ cup French or Italian salad dressing
½ teaspoon salt
Freshly ground black pepper to taste
1 cup sour cream (or low-fat yogurt for a low-calorie version)

The Garnish

8 or more Bibb lettuce leaves

For 16 Servings. The recipe may be doubled, but use only one and a half times the amount of dressing (1½ cups sour cream, 3 ounces salad dressing, ¾ teaspoon salt).

For 32 Servings. The recipe may be quadrupled, but use only two times the amount of dressing (2 cups sour cream, ½ cup salad dressing, 1 teaspoon salt).

Thaw the peas (if in a hurry, place the peas in a colander, run them under cold water, and drain thoroughly). Combine all the salad ingredients in a mixing bowl. Combine the dressing ingredients and fold gently into the salad mixture. Taste and correct the seasoning. Chill thoroughly. Serve individual mounds of salad on Bibb lettuce leaves arranged on a serving platter.

To Prepare in Advance. The salad can be covered and kept chilled no longer than 36 hours or the nuts will soften.

NEW YEAR'S BEANS
For 4½ quarts, or 32 servings

1 (55-ounce) can Brick Oven beans
1 (31-ounce) can pork and beans
1 (15-ounce) can black-eyed peas, drained
1 (15-ounce) can dark red kidney beans, drained
¼ pound salt pork, cut into ½-inch dice
4 medium onions, each cut in eighths
¾ cup firmly packed dark brown sugar
½ cup Dijon-style mustard (preferably Poupon label)
3 tablespoons Worcestershire sauce
6 to 8 good shakes Tabasco sauce
⅓ cup blackstrap molasses

Combine all the ingredients in a 5- or 6-quart ovenproof casserole or crock-pot and stir to blend. Bake at 350° for 2 hours ("high" on crock-pot), then reduce the heat to 200 to 250° ("low" on crock-pot) and continue cooking for 4 to 5 hours until thickened to your taste.

To Prepare in Advance. Store in the refrigerator for three days (or up to a week) or in the freezer for at least three months. If the mixture thickens too much when reheating, thin with a little water.

FRUIT PLATTER WITH PINEAPPLE CENTERPIECE

The Pineapple
1 large whole pineapple, with lush fronds
Flowers (daisies, mums, or other fresh flowers in season)
Parsley, to garnish

The Fruit Platter
(Use an assortment of at least three of the following fruits, depending on availability.)
2 baskets large strawberries
1 cantaloupe, cut, seeded, and flesh cut in wedges
1 honeydew melon, cut, seeded, and flesh cut in wedges
¼ watermelon, cut, seeded, and flesh cut in cubes
4 oranges (preferably navel), pared and sliced
2 papayas, pared, seeded, and cut in wedges
12 dates (see *Note 1*)
4 kiwi, pared and sliced
Bananas and apples (see *Note 2*)

Note 1: We are fond of the giant Medjool dates available at Hadley's near Palm Springs, California. They are available by mail order from several other sources listed in *The Complete Food Catalogue* by José Wilson and Arthur Leaman, published by Holt, Rinehart and Winston.

Note 2: Fruits that discolor after cutting, such as bananas and apples, should be dipped in fresh lemon juice or in Fruit Fresh, a powdered ascorbic acid (vitamin C), available in most supermarkets. Fruit Fresh, used in home canning, prevents fruit from darkening without affecting the flavor. Follow package directions.

For 16 Servings. One pineapple is sufficient, but double the amount of the fruits and arrange as described on a very large platter.

For 32 Servings. You may wish to prepare two identical platters, using two pineapples. A single platter, however, is easily replenished with fruit from the kitchen.

To make the pineapple, cut an even slice from the bottom of the pineapple so that it stands firmly in the center of the platter. Evenly cut a slice off the top near the fronds and set aside.

With a sharp knife remove the rind from the rest of the pineapple. Leave in the "eyes." Now study the peeled pineapple and cutting on the diagonal, use the tip of a sharp paring knife to cut thin, long V-shaped pineapple wedges to remove the eyes. The finished pineapple will be adorned with a series of spiral rows.

If the pineapple fronds are crushed, they can be revived by being held upside down under hot running water until they are soft. Reshape with your hands, then follow with a cold-water bath; trim the brown parts.

To provide height to your fruit platter, invert a champagne glass in the center of your serving platter. Top with the pineapple.

Weave fresh-cut flowers, such as daisies, into the fronds. Wreathe attractively with the cut fruits. Garnish the finished platter with parsley. Serve as soon as possible.

To Prepare in Advance. Prepare the pineapple, without the flowers, 24 hours ahead. Wrap loosely in damp paper towels and keep coiled. Insert flowers within 1 hour of serving and re-cover with towels until just before your guests arrive. If you have refrigerator space, fruits that do not darken on standing can be arranged on the platter up to 4 hours before serving. Garnish with parsley and cover the entire platter with damp paper towels to preserve freshness. Just before serving, remove the towels, and add the treated bananas or apples.

OUR BEST BUTTERMILK BISCUITS
For 16 biscuits

2 cups sifted all-purpose flour
2 tablespoons double-acting baking powder
2 teaspoons sugar
¼ teaspoon salt
⅛ teaspoon baking soda
1⅛ to 1¼ cups buttermilk
3 to 4 tablespoons vegetable oil

Preheat the oven to 500°. Combine the flour, baking powder, sugar, and salt in a medium mixing bowl. Stir the soda into 1⅛ cups buttermilk and combine with the dry ingredients, mixing well. If the mixture is dry, add the remaining ⅛ cup buttermilk. Turn the dough out onto a well-floured surface (we like to use a pastry cloth) and knead gently about five times.

With floured hands, press the dough into a patty ¾-inch thick. Using a 2-inch biscuit cutter (or the rim of a glass), cut out the biscuits. Without overflouring, press scraps of dough together to form a patty, and continue cutting until all the dough is used.

Dip each biscuit into the vegetable oil to coat completely. Arrange the biscuits, sides touching, in an 8-inch round cake pan or pie plate. Bake at 500° for 10 to 12 minutes until the biscuits are a delicate golden brown and no longer doughy inside. Serve immediately with butter and honey.

To Prepare in Advance. In the morning, set out the dry ingredients and the baking pan. Finish assembling 1 hour before your guests arrive and bake as close to serving time as possible—the biscuits are best when freshly baked. If necessary, you can bake them ahead, cover them with foil and reheat at 300° for 10 minutes, or until hot.

MUTTI'S VIENNESE CHEESECAKE

¾ cup dried currants or raisins
½ cup brandy
1 cup (4 ounces) blanched almonds
10 tablespoons (1¼ sticks) butter or margarine, at room temperature
1 cup sugar
2 teaspoons vanilla extract
5 eggs, separated and at room temperature
12 ounces cream cheese, at room temperature
Zest (yellow peel) of 1 lemon, finely chopped
¼ teaspoon cream of tartar, or 1 teaspoon freshly squeezed lemon juice

The Garnish

Powdered sugar
A long-stemmed rose or other flower of your choice

For 32 Servings. Some guests will eat little or no dessert. Three cheesecakes should be sufficient, or serve one or two in addition to an alternate dessert.

At least 24 hours (or up to a week) before making the cheesecake, soak the currants or raisins in brandy to cover. Set aside, covered, at room temperature.

Line a 12¾x 4¼x 2½-inch loaf pan (we use one made by Ekco) with aluminum foil. Coarsely grind the almonds in a food processor fitted with the steel blade or in an electric blender, ½ cup at a time, turning the machine on and off in short bursts. Set aside.

In a food processor fitted with the plastic blade or in the bowl of an electric mixer, combine the butter, sugar, egg yolks, cream cheese, and vanilla and beat until smooth. Stir in the ground almonds, currants or raisins (drain and reserve brandy for steeping more raisins or as flavoring), and lemon zest.

Beat the egg whites with either the cream of tartar or the lemon juice just until the whites do not slide when the bowl is tilted. Fold half the beaten whites into the cream cheese mixture thoroughly. Carefully fold in the remaining whites. Pour the batter into the foil-lined pan. Bake at 350° for about 1 hour, or until a toothpick inserted in the center comes out clean. Remove from the oven. The cheesecake will rise like a soufflé during the baking and will fall as it cools. When cool, turn out onto a long serving platter. With the back of a spoon, press powdered sugar through a sieve to lightly dust the top of the dessert. Top with a long-stemmed rose.

To Prepare in Advance. This dessert is easier to cut and improves in texture if made at least 24 hours before serving. In the Timetable, we suggest you make it three days in advance to lighten your buffet preparation chores. If tightly covered, it will keep up to three days at room temperature, a week in the refrigerator, or up to three months in the freezer. For best flavor, serve at room temperature.

PERFECT PUMPKIN PIE

The Crust

½ recipe Super-Flaky Pastry (see Recipes index), or your favorite recipe for 1, 9-inch pie crust

1 egg white, beaten

The Filling

2 eggs, plus 1 yolk

1½ cups pumpkin purée or canned pumpkin

¾ cup sugar

½ teaspoon salt

1 teaspoon ground cinnamon

½ teaspoon ground ginger

¼ teaspoon ground cloves

¼ cup brandy

¼ cup dark Jamaican rum

1¼ cups evaporated milk

The Topping

1 cup heavy cream (whipping cream)

¼ cup powdered sugar

1 teaspoon vanilla extract

Roll out the pastry on a lightly floured surface to a thickness of ⅜ inch. Trim it 1 inch wider than the diameter of the pan. Ease it into the pie pan and make a high rim of pastry around the rim; flute it decoratively. Brush the entire surface, including the rim, with the beaten egg white to "waterproof" the pastry. Chill until needed.

For the top of the pie, make and bake 11 "leaves" (described under Pastry Leaves and Flowers in the Garnishes appendix) from the pastry trimmings. Eight leaves will be used around the edges and 3 in the center.

Preheat the oven to 425°. In a large mixing bowl, beat the eggs, pumpkin, sugar, salt, and spices until very well blended. Beat in the brandy and rum, followed by the evaporated milk. Pour the filling into the prepared shell. Bake at 425° for 15 minutes, then reduce the oven temperature to 350°. Continue baking for 45 to 50 minutes, or until a knife inserted into the center of the pie comes out clean. Cool on a rack for at least 1 hour before cutting. Top with the "leaves" just before serving.

To make the topping, whip the cream until it holds a soft shape when mounded. Press the powdered sugar through a kitchen strainer with the back of a spoon to remove any lumps and beat it into the cream with the vanilla extract. Serve a dollop of whipped cream with each slice.

To Prepare in Advance. Like most pies, this pumpkin pie tastes best if served the day it is baked, preferably still warm from the oven. It can be made up to three days before serving. Store, covered, in the refrigerator. For best flavor, heat 7 to 10 minutes at 300° before serving. The topping can be whipped the morning of the buffet and stored in a serving bowl in the refrigerator.

ENCORES

The next day invite some friends over for ham sandwiches, pea salad, Hot Brie, and whatever leftovers you want to share. Everything will still be delicious, except the biscuits, which are not very appetizing the next day, and the punch, which may be too watered down. When your second party is over, freeze leftover beans and cheesecake to use another day.

Olde English Roast Beef Buffet

Menu

Christmas Punch Bowl or Sipping Sherry

Sparkling Apple Juice

Butter-Roasted Pecans

Slow-Roasted Beef

Châteauneuf du-Pape or *Petite Sirah*

Horseradish Mousse

Scalloped Oysters

Gulliver's Creamed Corn

Tomatoes Noël

Purée of Peas Pépin

Hot Buttered Bread Ring

Brandied Chocolate Fruitcake

Hazelnut Meringue Torte with
Apricot Filling

Coffee and Tea

OLDE ENGLISH
ROAST BEEF BUFFET

T he center of attention in this buffet is our tall parsleyed Christmas tree centerpiece, towering over the abundant display food. The punch bowl, too, is in the spirit of Christmas with its red and green garnish of floating strawberries stemmed with sprigs of mint (one of Paul's creations). Frances Pelham's Sipping Sherry is an alternate. Several bottles of iced sparkling apple juice are provided for the children and others who prefer nonalcoholic drinks.

There is so much food for this buffet that we have dispensed with the appetizer. The small bowls of buttery nuts should suffice as nibblers.

We were introduced to the Slow-Roasted Beef through our friend, Mary Erpelding. Her method minimizes shrinkage and loss of juices. Our creamed corn version is based on a recipe we received from Gulliver's, a chain of California restaurants justifiably famous for their creamed corn.

Jacques Pépin, the *House Beautiful* chef, fills small pastry shells *(barquettes)* with a brilliant green purée, made with peas, and tops each shell with a poached egg and a very light hollandaise. For this buffet, the purée is served as is.

The Hot Buttered Bread Ring, called "Monkey Bread," pulls apart with the fingers for easy serving and requires no additional butter.

We are grateful to two other friends for the dessert recipes. Natalie Haughton, who is the food editor of *The Valley News* in California (for which Paul writes a weekly column) gifted us one Christmas with one of her Brandied Chocolate Fruitcakes. Along with the fruitcake, we offer Marlene Sorosky's rich and luscious meringue torte, a recipe from one of her cooking classes, "La Cuisine de Marlene."

THE TABLE SETTINGS

This is an elaborate, single-line, seated buffet. Knife and fork are required; silverware and napkins are on preset tables. Refreshments, desserts, and beverages are served separately.

Centerpieces

The Buffet Table. To make the vegetable Christmas tree base, you will need two rectangular pieces of 1-inch-thick Styrofoam, one smaller than the other; a Styrofoam cone; a champagne glass; white glue; and

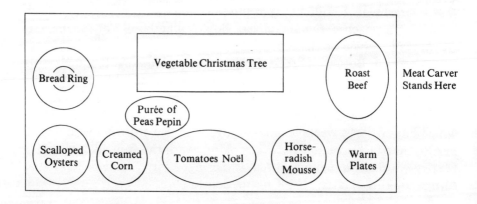

"Stickum" (sticky tape). To decorate the tree, you will need hairpins, several yards of ribbon, double-ended toothpicks, parsley, cherry tomatoes, pattypan squash (trimmed and sliced to resemble a star). To cover the base, you will need sphagnum moss, small green pine boughs, pine cones, assorted nuts and vegetables.

Glue the small rectangle to the center of the large one. Wrap the tape around the lip of the glass and place the glass upside down in the center of the base. Press tape around the base of the glass (now at the top) and fasten the Styrofoam cone securely in the center with the tape.

To decorate the tree, cut clusters of parsley, leaving 2-inch stems. Begin at the bottom and fasten the clusters to the cone (stems up) with hairpins, completely filling the tree and covering stems as you go. Fasten a few bunches at the top (stems down). Insert the toothpicks decoratively into the cone and stick tomatoes on them. Make bows and place over each tomato. Spear the star-shaped squash with a toothpick and place at the top. Cover the base of the tree with a thin layer of moss. Cover with the vegetables, nuts, pine cones, and boughs.

With the exception of the bows, the trees can be prepared the morning of the party. Spray the parsley with a mister, wrap in a damp tea towel, and store in a cool, dark place. Just before guests arrive, spray again and add the bows.

The Dining Tables. Make the centerpieces as described in the Exotic Curry and Chutney Buffet, using pears for the fruit. For each centerpiece, wind a handful of sphagnum moss around your fingers to form a nest. Fill the next with a few artificial birds, purchased in a florist shop, and place on the top of the tree. You now have "A Partridge in a Pear Tree."

SCENTED CINNAMON STICK BUNDLES

To make 8 bundles, you will need 1 pound of long cinnamon sticks, 4 yards of ribbon, and ¼ ounce oil of cinnamon, optional (available at well-stocked pharmacies).

Break the cinnamon into 5- or 6-inch lengths—they do not need to be even. Divide the sticks into eight bundles and tie each one around the middle with a ribbon; make a bow. For a stronger cinnamon scent, sprinkle each bundle lightly with a few drops of oil of cinnamon. For the name cards, cut plain 3x5-inch index cards into thirds. Write each guest's name at the top of each card and insert into a cinnamon bundle. Make the bundles whenever convenient. The aroma from the oil of cinnamon won't last long, so add it within 24 hours of the party.

TIMETABLE

Six Weeks Before the Party. Make the fruitcakes. Make the homemade mincemeat for the Tomatoes Noël if you are not purchasing it ready-made. Also prepare the cinnamon stick bundles, Sipping Sherry, and Butter-Roasted Pecans.

Three Days Before the Party. Stud the tangerines with the cloves for the punch; steep them in the orange liqueur.

The Day Before the Party. Enlist as much help as you can to make the Horseradish Mousse, the meringue layers for the torte and the soaked apricots for the filling, the stuffing mixture for the oysters, and the ice ring and mint-speared strawberries for the punch. Glaze the fruit-cake(s). Weigh the roast beef and plan the oven timing. Make the orange roses to decorate the mousse. Chill the champagne and sparkling apple juice.

The Morning of the Party. Prepare the Tomatoes Noël. Prepare the beef for roasting; set a timer to remind you when it is to go in the oven, and place it in the oven at that time. Within 8 hours of serving, assemble the bread ring and the corn; refrigerate, ready to bake before serving. Assemble and decorate the torte; chill until serving time. Unmold and decorate the Horseradish Mousse. Place pecans in serving dishes on coffee tables and other places around the room.

If you have two ovens, all the accompaniments to the roast beef (the oysters, corn, tomatoes, and bread ring) may be baked in the second oven while the roast beef stays warm in the first. If a single oven must suffice, remove the roast beef from the oven when done; cover it with foil, and place in a warm place. Raise the oven temperature to 375° and cook the accompaniments for 35 minutes.

COUNTDOWN

45 minutes before guests arrive:	Prepare the purée of peas. Keep warm in a double boiler.
	Slice one fruitcake and arrange the slices around an uncut fruitcake.
15 minutes before guests arrive:	Unmold the ice ring into the punch bowl and add all the punch ingredients, except champagne.
	Assemble Scalloped Oysters.

	Set out decanter of sherry and place bottles of sparkling apple juice or ice.
	Start coffee and tea.
As guests arrive:	Add champagne to punch and set out.
35 minutes before serving:	Bake bread ring and oysters in the same oven (375°).
10 minutes before serving:	Place the corn and tomatoes in the oven.
	Warm serving plate for roast.
	Garnish the dishes and place all main-course items on the buffet table.
At serving time:	Brown the corn.
	Announce the feast.

RECIPES

CHRISTMAS PUNCH BOWL
For 8 servings

 1 tangerine, studded with whole cloves as elaborately as you like
 ½ cup Triple Sec, Grand Marnier, or Cointreau
 8 to 12 fresh strawberries
 8 to 12 sprigs of fresh mint (or parsley)
 Syrup (see *Note*)
 2 bottles (fifths) champagne, chilled
 Minted Ice Ring or Fern Ice Ring (optional, see Ice Rings in Garnishes appendix)

For 32 Servings. Recipe may be quadrupled, but 2 or 3 clove-studded tangerines will suffice.

Note: You may wish to sweeten the punch if the liqueur you have chosen is not sweet enough. Granulated sugar won't dissolve in alcohol, so use a simple syrup: equal parts sugar and water simmered together for 5 minutes. About ⅛ cup of syrup per fifth of champagne is enough.

Place the clove-studded tangerine in a small bowl with the orange liqueur. Cover tightly to prevent evaporation and steep at room temperature at least 4 hours.

Spear mint leaves into the strawberries in the following manner: With a knife, split a wooden skewer at the blunt end about 1-inch deep. Insert a sprig of mint in the slit. With the opposite end spear the skewer through the frond of a strawberry and out the bottom. As the skewer is pulled all the way through, it will leave the mint sprig sticking out of the frond. Repeat with the remaining strawberries.

To make the punch, place the tangerine and orange liqueur (Triple Sec, Grand Marnier, or Cointreau) in a pitcher or punch bowl with an ice ring (double the ingredients if using a punch bowl). Add the mint-speared strawberries and pour in the chilled champagne. Taste for sweetness and add simple syrup if needed. Cheers!

To Prepare in Advance. The clove-studded tangerine can marinate in the liqueur for several days. Prepare the strawberries up to 24 hours ahead, wrap carefully in damp paper towels, and refrigerate until serving time. Then combine all components and serve.

SIPPING SHERRY
For 1 quart, or up to 16 small servings

    1 bottle (fifth) cream sherry (see *Note*)
    A long spiral of zest (orange peel) from a large orange
    6 allspice berries

Note: Frances Pelham, from whom this recipe came, prefers Llords and Elwood's "Judge's Secret" cream sherry for this recipe. It is reasonably priced and has a smooth flavor.

Combine the ingredients in a crystal decanter or bottle. Allow the sherry to mellow at room temperature for at least a week before serving.

To Prepare in Advance. Make at least one week ahead. It will keep indefinitely if stored in a cool place.

BUTTER-ROASTED PECANS

4 cups pecan halves
2 to 4 ounces (½ to 1 stick) butter or margarine, melted
2 teaspoons coarse salt (kosher salt)
¼ teaspoon freshly ground black pepper or more, to taste

Preheat the oven to 350°. Toss the pecan halves in the melted butter and place them in a single layer in a shallow baking pan. Roast them in the oven for 15 to 20 minutes, stirring often to prevent burning. They must be watched carefully toward the end of the cooking time so that they do not brown too much. Remove the baking pan from the oven and use a slotted spoon to transfer the nuts to a large brown grocery bag. (Save the butter remaining in the pan to drizzle over vegetables.) Sprinkle the nuts with the salt and pepper and shake in the bag to coat them evenly. Place in serving bowls. These nuts are best when served warm or at room temperature.

To Prepare in Advance. The roasted nuts will keep for weeks if stored in an airtight container in the refrigerator, or they can be made and frozen three months in advance. Serve at room temperature or slightly warm.

SLOW-ROASTED BEEF

3- or 4-pound boneless roast cut from the center of a standing rib
   (see *Note*), at room temperature
1 clove garlic, cut in half
Freshly ground black pepper

The Garnish

Fresh watercress

For 32 Servings. A 10-pound roast or two 5-pound roasts should be sufficient, but roast extra meat to avoid worrying about whether you will have enough.

Note: The cut may be called Eye of the Prime Rib or a Spencer Roast. Because it is boneless, it will cut very easily.

Preheat your oven to 225°. (Because oven thermostats can be way off, keep an oven thermometer in your oven at all times to be sure of accurate temperatures.)

Rub the roast with the cut garlic clove and a generous sprinkling of black pepper. (Never salt meat before roasting: Salt draws out the juices.) Place the roast, fat side up, in a roasting pan on a rack. Insert a meat thermometer into the center. Be sure it is imbedded in lean meat, not fat. Without opening the oven door, roast the meat for 30 to 40 minutes per pound until the meat thermometer registers 135° for rare meat or 145° for medium. Remove the roast from the oven and transfer to a warm platter. This roast can be carved immediately and does not need to "rest." Surround with fresh watercress. You might wish to carve the first slice for each guest at the beginning of the buffet. Guests can help themselves the second time around.

To Prepare in Advance. The roast can be kept in a very low oven (130°) up to 6 hours. To maintain the same degree of doneness, do not let the oven temperature exceed the internal temperature of the meat.

Afterthought. There are no drippings—all the juices stay in the meat. This roasting method is also superb for leg of lamb.

HORSERADISH MOUSSE
    ¼ cup cold water
    ½ package (1½ teaspoons) plain gelatin
    ¼ cup mayonnaise
    2 tablespoons grated or minced onion
    ⅓ cup fresh or bottled grated horseradish (see *Note*)
    ½ teaspoon salt
    ¼ teaspoon Worcestershire sauce
    ⅛ teaspoon white pepper or a few dashes cayenne pepper
    1 cup heavy cream (whipping cream)

The Garnish
    1 tablespoon minced parsley
    Small bunch watercress
    An Orange Rose (see Lemon or Orange Rose in Garnishes appendix)

Note: Bottled horseradish loses strength and flavor rapidly, even if refrigerated.

Oil a 2- or 3-cup mold or spray with nonstick cooking spray. Place the cold water in the top of a double boiler. Sprinkle the gelatin over the water and set aside to soften for 5 minutes. Meanwhile, combine the mayonnaise, onion, horseradish, and seasonings. In the large bowl of an electric mixer, whip the cream until it holds a soft shape; do not overbeat. Gently fold in the mayonnaise mixture.

Set the pan of softened gelatin over a pan of simmering water; stir until the gelatin is syrupy. Cool a few seconds, then pour it into the cream mixture, folding rapidly but gently until thoroughly blended. Pour into the prepared mold. Tap the bottom of the mold lightly on the counter or table to settle the contents. Press a piece of plastic wrap into the surface and refrigerate at least 3 hours.

To unmold, insert a dull knife gently up around the side of the mold. Place a serving plate upside down over it and, grasping the plate and mold firmly together, quickly invert them. The mousse should slide out easily. Or use Paul's quick method for unmolding (see Molds in Garnishes appendix). Garnish with a sprinkling of minced parsley and a small bed of watercress topped with a Lemon or Orange Rose. Serve chilled.

To Prepare in Advance. Make up to 24 hours before serving. Unmold within 4 hours of serving and keep chilled.

SCALLOPED OYSTERS
    12 tablespoons (1½ sticks) butter
    2½ cups crumbled dry herb-flavored stuffing mix
    3 tablespoons minced parsley
    1 quart (about 40) freshly shucked oysters
    ¼ cup heavy cream (whipping cream)
    Salt
    Freshly ground black pepper

For 32 Servings. A triple recipe should be sufficient; some guests will not eat oysters. Use one or two baking dishes; do not have more than two layers of oysters.

Preheat the oven to 375°. Melt the butter in a medium-size saucepan; add the stuffing mix and parsley. Toss to thoroughly coat all of the stuffing with the butter. Cover the bottom of a shallow baking dish with one third of the stuffing mixture. Arrange half the oysters over the stuffing; sprinkle lightly with salt and a generous amount of freshly ground pepper; pour in half the cream. Repeat the layering in the same order. Top with the remaining stuffing and bake for 30 minutes. Serve immediately.

To Prepare in Advance. The stuffing mixture can be prepared the day before and stored, covered, in the refrigerator. For best results, assemble the dish within 1 hour of baking.

GULLIVER'S CREAMED CORN

2 (20 ounces *each*) packages frozen corn
2 cups (1 pint) light cream (half-and-half)
2 tablespoons sugar
1½ teaspoons salt
Good dash cayenne
Good dash Worcestershire sauce
2 tablespoons butter or margarine, softened or melted
2 tablespoons all-purpose flour

The Topping

2 tablespoons grated Parmesan cheese
1 tablespoon chopped parsley

In a heavy 3-quart saucepan, combine the corn, light cream, sugar, salt, cayenne, and Worcestershire sauce. Bring to a boil, lower the heat, and simmer for 5 minutes. Meanwhile, blend the butter and flour together to form a paste. Blend the butter-flour mixture (known in culinary terms as *beurre manié*) into the corn mixture. Stir over low heat until thickened. Transfer to a shallow, heatproof baking dish or gratin dish. Evenly sprinkle the Parmesan over the top. Place the dish under the broiler until the topping is nicely browned. Sprinkle with chopped parsley before serving.

To Prepare in Advance. The dish can be prepared and cooked up to 8 hours before serving. If refrigerated, bring to room temperature and reheat at 300° to 375° (whatever temperature is convenient) for about 10 to 15 minutes to warm through. Brown and garnish as directed above.

TOMATOES NOËL

8 firm, medium-size tomatoes

The Filling

4 ounces wild rice
1 tablespoon salt
¼ pound well-seasoned bulk pork sausage (see *Note*)

¼ cup minced onion
½ cup mincemeat (homemade or purchased)
¼ cup sliced almonds
2 tablespoons minced parsley
½ teaspoon salt
¼ teaspoon freshly ground black pepper

The Garnish

1 tablespoon sliced almonds
Minced parsley

Note: Taste the sausage after it is fully cooked. If it is not well-seasoned, add a pinch of each of the following: marjoram, sage, summer savory, thyme, and black pepper.

To prepare the tomatoes, cut an even slice off the stem ends. Use a small kitchen spoon such as a serrated grapefruit spoon to scoop out the centers. Sprinkle the interiors lightly with salt and turn upside down on paper towels to drain for at least 15 minutes. Set aside.

For the filling, place the wild rice in a kitchen strainer and run it under cold running water until the water runs clear. Transfer the rice to a pot and cover with cold water to a depth of 2 inches. Add the salt. Bring to a boil and simmer about 30 minutes until the rice is tender. Drain and cool.

Meanwhile, cook the sausage with the minced onion in a skillet, mashing it constantly with a wooden spoon to break up any lumps, and cook until no trace of pink remains in the meat. Taste and correct seasoning if necessary as indicated in the *Note*. Drain off fat. Stir in the wild rice and the remaining filling ingredients.

Fill the tomatoes with the meat mixture, mounding it slightly. Arrange the tomatoes, sides touching, in a lightly buttered baking dish large enough to hold them without crowding. Heat at 325° to 375° for 15 minutes, or long enough to heat the filling. Decoratively sprinkle each tomato with sliced almonds and parsley.

To Prepare in Advance. The filling can be made several days ahead or frozen up to two months in advance. Prepare and stuff the tomato shells within 12 hours of serving. Refrigerate, covered, in the baking dish. Bring dish to room temperature, heat, and garnish.

PURÉE OF PEAS PÉPIN

    2 cups water
    1 (10-ounce) package frozen "petite" peas
    ¾ teaspoon salt
    2 tablespoons sweet butter
    ¼ teaspoon ground white pepper
    Dash sugar

Place the water in a small saucepan and bring to a boil. Add the frozen peas and ¼ teaspoon of the salt and bring to a boil. Reduce heat and simmer, uncovered, for 3 to 4 minutes until the peas are tender. Drain thoroughly. Place the hot peas in the container of a food processor fitted with the steel blade, along with all the other ingredients and the remaining salt. Process for at least 1 minute. The mixture should not be completely smooth: The skins from the peas give it an interesting texture and a bright green color.

If you do not have a processor, simply serve the peas plain—same taste, different appearance.

To Prepare in Advance. The purée can be kept warm for at least 1 hour in a double boiler over hot, not boiling, water. If heated longer, the peas will lose their bright green color.

HOT BUTTERED BREAD RING

For up to 16 servings

    10 tablespoons (1¼ sticks) butter or margarine
    3 (8 ounces *each*) packages Pillsbury Butterflake refrigerator rolls

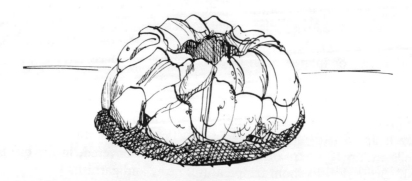

Preheat the oven to 375°. Melt the butter in a small saucepan. Remove from heat and cool for a few minutes. Separate the rolls and dip them, one at a time, in the cooled butter. Arrange the rolls casually in a Bundt or other 12-cup ring mold. (Do not use an angelfood cake pan or the butter will leak out during baking.) Bake for 25 minutes; do not overbake. Let rest in the pan for 5 minutes, then turn out onto a serving platter. Serve immediately.

To Prepare in Advance. Prepare up to the point of baking. Refrigerate up to 24 hours. Bake just before serving.

BRANDIED CHOCOLATE FRUITCAKE
For two 9x5x3-inch loaves of 16 servings each, or four 7¾x3-5/8x2¼-inch loaves of 8 servings each

    1 cup (8 ounces) diced candied pineapple
    ½ cup (4 ounces) candied cherries, halved
    1 cup seedless raisins
    ½ cup brandy
    4 squares (4 ounces) unsweetened chocolate
    12 tablespoons (1½ sticks) butter or margarine
    1½ cups sugar
    6 large eggs, separated
    2 cups sifted all-purpose flour
    1 teaspoon baking powder
    3 cups coarsely chopped pecans or walnuts

The Glaze (optional)
    1½ cups powdered sugar
    3 to 4 tablespoons heavy cream (whipping cream) or light cream
      (half-and-half)
    ¼ teaspoon almond extract
    Candied red cherries

Combine the candied fruits, raisins, and brandy in a small bowl; cover and let it stand for several hours or overnight. Drain the fruit; reserve the brandy. You will need ⅓ cup brandy. If the fruit has absorbed most of it, add enough brandy to give you the necessary amount. Set the fruits and brandy aside.

Line the loaf pans with brown wrapping paper that has been greased on both sides with oil. Melt the chocolate in the top of a double boiler placed over gently boiling water, and set aside to cool.

Preheat the oven to 250°. Cream the butter or margarine in an electric mixing bowl. Gradually add 1 cup of the sugar and blend well. Beat in the egg yolks, two at a time, beating after each addition. Stop the motor often to scrape down the sides of the bowl with a rubber spatula. When the egg yolks are thoroughly mixed in, beat in the cooled chocolate.

Resift the flour with the baking powder and add it to the batter alternately with the reserved brandy. Stir in the fruits and nuts.

Beat the egg whites until they just begin to hold their shape; then slowly add the remaining ½ cup sugar, beating until soft peaks form. Fold about one fourth of the whites into the batter and then gently but thoroughly fold in the remaining whites. Turn into the prepared pans.

Place the filled pans into shallow pans. Pour in enough boiling water to come about halfway up the sides of the loaf pans. Bake the loaves until the cakes test done or until a toothpick inserted in the center comes out clean (about 1½ hours for the small loaves, 2½ hours for the large ones). Cool the fruitcakes for 15 minutes, then remove from the pans. Pour a few tablespoons of brandy over each cake; cool thoroughly. Wrap them individually in plastic wrap or cheesecloth, then in foil. Store for 6 to 8 weeks in the refrigerator before serving; sprinkle the cakes with brandy two or three times during this period.

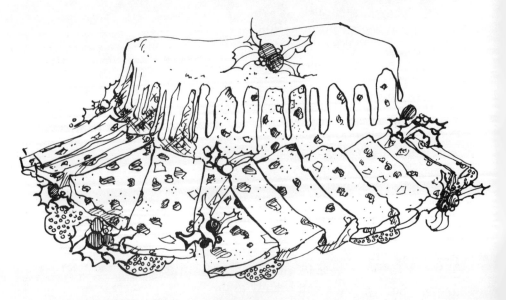

Within 24 hours of serving, glaze and decorate the fruitcakes, if desired. To prepare the glaze, beat the powdered sugar, cream, and almond extract until smooth. Spread the glaze over the top of the cakes and let it drip down the sides. Arrange the candied red cherry halves over the tops.

To serve, place one glazed fruitcake in the center of a large platter. Cut another cake into thin slices and overlap the slices around the uncut cake.

To Prepare in Advance. Fruitcakes are best if allowed to age in the refrigerator for at least six weeks. They can be stored (and in the process, improve) for years in the refrigerator. Occasionally unwrap them and sprinkle with a tablespoon or so of brandy. The cakes can also be frozen, but refrigerator storage is best.

HAZELNUT MERINGUE TORTE WITH APRICOT FILLING

2 cups (½ pound) shelled hazelnuts, finely ground (see *Note*)
6 egg whites, at room temperature
1½ cups superfine sugar
½ teaspoon white vinegar
1½ teaspoons vanilla extract

The Filling

4 ounces dried apricots
¼ cup sugar
1 tablespoon freshly squeezed lemon juice
1 cup (½ pint) heavy cream (whipping cream)
2 tablespoons powdered sugar

The Garnish

½ cup (2 ounces) whole hazelnuts

Note: There are two easy methods for grinding nuts. In an electric blender put ½ cup of nuts at a time in the container, cover, and run the motor at medium for a few seconds. Or, place all the nuts at once in the container of a food processor and process with the steel blade until finely ground.

Cover the apricots with water and soak them overnight to soften.

Spread the ground hazelnuts on a baking sheet and toast in a 350° oven for about 5 minutes until lightly browned. Watch carefully so that they do not burn. Let the nuts cool while you prepare the meringue. Increase oven temperature to 375°.

Beat the egg whites at low speed until foamy. Increase speed to high and beat until soft peaks form when the beater is lifted. Gradually add the sugar, a tablespoon at a time, beating until very stiff peaks form. Beat in the vinegar and vanilla, then gently fold in the ground hazelnuts until thoroughly combined. Evenly divide the meringue mixture into two greased and floured 9-inch round cake pans; smooth out the top. Bake for 30 minutes or until lightly browned and the top is firm; do not overbake. Cool for 10 minutes; turn out of the pans onto racks to cool.

To finish the filling, pour off all but 3 to 4 tablespoons of the water in which the apricots were soaking. Add the sugar and lemon juice. Transfer to a saucepan and simmer, covered, about 30 minutes until very soft. Mash with a fork or potato masher until the mixture is fairly smooth. Cool. Beat the cream with powdered sugar until stiff. Fold thoroughly into the apricot mixture.

Assemble within 8 hours of serving. Place one meringue layer on a serving plate. Spread with about one fourth of the apricot cream. Top with a second meringue layer. Spread with another thin layer of cream. With the remaining cream spoon small dabs in place or put the cream into a pastry bag fitted with a wide star tip and pipe rosettes around the edge. Top each rosette with a whole hazelnut.

To Prepare in Advance. The apricot mixture can be frozen several months in advance or refrigerated up to four days. The meringue layers should be made one day ahead and stored on plates, loosely covered with plastic wrap. They are fragile. The torte should not be assembled more than 8 hours in advance. Assembling it earlier than 8 hours makes the torte soggy. Refrigerate until dessert time.

PEAR TART WITH POMEGRANATE SEEDS
For 8 to 10 servings

A 9-inch tart pan or flan ring lined with Pâte Sucrée (recipe follows)
⅓ cup coarsely ground blanched almonds (optional, see *Note*)
4 to 5 large pears (see *Note*)

¾ cup (6 ounces) apricot preserves, puréed in the blender
2 tablespoons sugar
2 tablespoons (¼ stick) butter or margarine
1 to 2 tablespoons pear brandy, Grand Marnier, or cognac

The Garnish
Seeds of ⅓ ripe pomegranate

Note: Firm pears give the best results. If the pears are very ripe and juicy, strew the ground nuts over the crust before filling. The nuts will absorb the juices and prevent a soggy tart.

Preheat the oven to 400°. Trim the stems from the pears. Cut off the necks, peel, and chop coarsely. Set aside. Peel the remaining portion of the pears, cut in half, and remove the core. Cut into ¼-inch crosswise slices.

Use a pastry brush to brush the inside of the pastry shell with ⅓ cup of the puréed apricot preserves—this will "waterproof" the pastry. Mound the chopped pear trimmings on the bottom of the shell. Overlap most of the slices around the outer edges of the tart. Arrange the remaining pear slices in the center. Sprinkle the sugar evenly over the top of the tart; dot with small bits of butter or margarine. Bake the tart in the lower third of the oven for 65 to 75 minutes until the pears are browned and the crust is baked and golden around the edges. Mix the remaining apricot preserves with the pear brandy, Grand Marnier, or cognac to make a brushable glaze and brush it gently over the entire surface of the tart. Cool for at least 1 hour before cutting. Sprinkle the entire surface with pomegranate seeds just before serving. Serve warm or at room temperature.

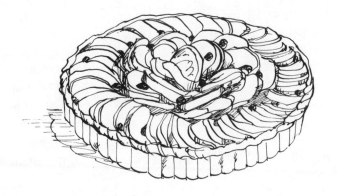

To Prepare in Advance. Fruit tarts are best when made the same day they are served. Leave at room temperature until serving time. Refrigeration turns them soggy.

PÂTE SUCRÉE
For a 9- or 10-inch tart

This sweet and cookie-like dough is good with all fruit tarts. It is crumbly and a bit difficult to wrap around a rolling pin and place into the tart pan, but don't worry. If you press it into the pan, it won't suffer from being overhandled as most pie doughs do.

1½ cups all-purpose flour
10 tablespoons (1¼ sticks) butter, cut in pieces
¼ cup sugar
⅛ teaspoon salt
1 large egg, lightly beaten

To make this dough in a food processor, follow our instructions for Super-Flaky Pie Crust (see Recipes index).

To make it on a cutting board or marble slab, place the flour in the center of your work surface. Make a well in the center and add the remaining ingredients. Work the dough together with your fingers. It will be crumbly. Gather the dough into a single mass. With the heel, which is the coolest part of your hand, take a piece of dough the size of a golf ball and press down, fingers pointed up, and rub away from you about 10 inches across the work surface. Repeat until all the dough has been worked. Gather the dough into a ball and repeat the operation once or twice more until it is well blended.

Roll the dough into a 12-inch circle about ¼-inch thick. Wrap around a rolling pin, place over the pan, and unroll carefully, easing the dough into the pan. With your fingers, build up the thickness of the dough on the sides of the pan 3/8 inch. Trim the overhang. Using your fingers, press the dough on the sides to form a rim higher than the edge of the pan. Make a decorative border by pressing the rim on an angle with the end of a wooden spoon or with the tines of a fork. Chill until needed.

To Prepare in Advance. The shell can be frozen two months in advance.

ENCORES

Use up the pears from the centerpieces before they overripen. What remains uneaten can go into an elegant open-face pear tart strewn with pomegranate seeds (recipe follows).

Leftover roast beef is delicious served cold. Serve it sliced with horseradish mousse or turn it into hearty roast beef sandwiches. We've never had much luck reheating the slices, but, of course, they do make a good hash. The oysters won't keep; however, we doubt that you will have any left over to deal with. The corn and bread can be reheated the next day for family fare. Any remaining punch and peas will lose their freshness, as will the torte and tomatoes, so toss them out or eat them up. The fruitcake will keep just about forever. If one remains uncut, scrape off the icing, sprinkle with brandy and rewrap in foil; refrigerate.

We've never had any buttery pecans left, but if we did they would keep for weeks in the refrigerator in an airtight container.

FINGER-FOOD BUFFET

Menu

Wine or Open Bar

Appetizer Quiche Lorraine

Cooked Artichokes
or
Basket of Raw Vegetables
with Marjorie's Dip

Freshly Cooked Shrimp with Pesto Dip

Kielbasa in Dark Beer with Tarragon

Round Rye Sandwich Loaf

Platter of Assorted Cheeses and Crackers

Butter-Roasted Pecans

Chafing Dish Chili with Condiments

Assorted Finger-Food Sweets
Miniature Strawberry Tarts
Sunshine Squares
Black Bottom Cups
Macadamia Nut Candy Mauna Kea
Creamy Caramels with Walnuts

Coffee and Tea

CASUAL OPEN HOUSE
FINGER-FOOD BUFFET

The underlying themes of this informal "get-together" are relaxation and fun—encouraged to a great measure by the steady, tempting flow of food, both hot and cold.

Crowds ebbing and flowing through your home can keep you busy, especially if you have taken on the responsibility of both the kitchen and the bar. Because it is casual, you might decide not to have a bartender and instead have a guitarist strum for a few hours.

An open house means guests arrive at odd times. Even so, the management of a steady flow of hot food from the kitchen might be frustrating. One of the ways we solved this problem was to improvise on an idea of James Beard's: Sliced ovals of Polish kielbasa sausage brought to a simmer in dark beer laced with tarragon are passed on toothpicks throughout the evening. Bowls of them placed in various areas disperse hungry nibblers around the buffet table.

The quiche is a popular appetizer for a large group, or it may be cut into larger squares for an easy brunch or luncheon main course.

The tangy flavor of Marj Berger's dip for the artichokes also complements raw vegetables. Freshly cooked Shrimp with Pesto Dip strikes an Italian note. The rye bread for the sandwich loaf can be ordered from a bakery and the sliced meat fillings purchased from a delicatessen, so the sandwich loaf becomes a matter of assembling.

Near the end of the party, present the elegant Chafing Dish Chili to wake up your guests' appetites.

The recipe for the Basket of Raw Vegetables appears in the Elegant Open House Buffet, the Butter-Roasted Pecans in the Olde English Roast Beef Buffet, and the Finger-Food Sweets in the Exotic Curry and Chutney Buffet.

THE TABLE SETTINGS

This is a semielaborate, single-line, serve-yourself buffet. No silverware is required, except spoons for the chili. Cocktails or wine is served at the bar. Coffee and tea are served separately.

Centerpieces

Buffet and Dining Tables. For each centerpiece, place a head of red-leaf lettuce in a shallow basket. Around it arrange a colorful assortment of vegetables: yellow crookneck squash, red bell peppers, eggplant, leeks, heads of garlic, long green chiles, zucchini, carrots, red cabbage, cauliflower, radishes, and tomatoes. Spray with nonstick cooking spray to give the vegetables a sheen. The centerpieces can be prepared (without the lettuce) two or three days earlier and kept in a cool, dark place. Add the lettuce just before guests arrive.

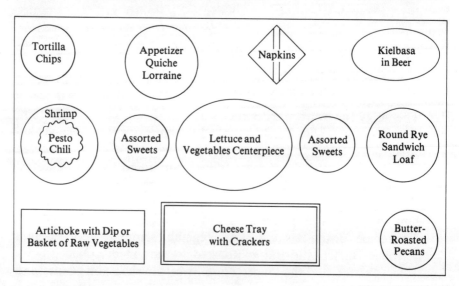

TIMETABLE

Several Weeks Before the Party. If you want a bartender to supervise an open bar, make the necessary arrangements. Prepare the Butter-Roasted Pecans, creamy caramels, and macadamia nut candy and store in a cool place. Prepare and freeze the chili, Black Bottom Cups, Sunshine Squares, and the pastry shells for the Miniature Strawberry Tarts.

Four Days Before the Party. Make Marjorie's Dip. Line the quiche pan with crust; store in the freezer until the day of the party—it won't require thawing.

Three Days Before the Party. Map out your battle plan. Do your marketing. Shop at a cheese shop for excellent quality and unusual cheeses. Wrap them in airtight plastic wrap. Prepare identifying flags to spear into the top of each one.

Two Days Before the Party. Make the Round Rye Sandwich Loaf. Wrap in a damp tea towel and refrigerate in a plastic bag. Make the Pesto Dip.

The Day Before the Party. Cook the artichokes for the dip. Cut, wrap, and refrigerate all the vegetables. Thaw the chili; prepare the condiments and refrigerate. Cook the kielbasa in the beer and marinate it in the refrigerator. Cook, peel, and devein the shrimp and keep chilled. Make the glaze for the tarts. Thaw the frozen dessert items. Wash parsley for garnishing, wrap in paper towels and plastic bag, and refrigerate.

The Morning of the Party. If you are on schedule, you will meet the day with anticipation. Fill and bake the quiche. Cool, cut, and leave at room temperature. Make the filling for the tarts. Within 6 hours of serving, fill and glaze them. Keep chilled.

COUNTDOWN

1½ hours before guests arrive: Arrange the cheese tray, insert flags, and set out with crackers.
Arrange platters of assorted sweets.
Put pecans in serving bowls in various locations.

1 hour before guests arrive:	Place the chili in a crock-pot on "low" or in a saucepan for stove-top heating later.
	Arrange shrimp around dip, cover with plastic wrap, and chill.
	Place glass of dip in hollow of artichokes or in basket of raw vegetables to come to room temperature.
30 minutes before guests arrive:	Check the bar setup and fill ice buckets.
	Garnish and set out the sandwich loaf.
15 minutes before guests arrive:	Prepare coffee and tea.
	Heat kielbasa and set out.
	Warm quiche and its serving plates.
As guests arrive:	Set out warm plates of quiche.
	Remove towels from shrimp and set out.
About 1 hour before guests depart:	Clear away some of the appetizers to serve chili and condiments.

RECIPES

APPETIZER QUICHE LORRAINE - *15" x 10½" pan*

For 50 to 60 appetizer-size pieces, or 12 to 16 main-course servings

Super-Flaky Pastry (see Recipes index) or use your favorite recipe
  for a two-crust 9-inch pie
1 pound bacon, sliced
2 tablespoons butter or margarine (optional)
1 medium onion, minced
8 large eggs
¼ cup freshly grated Parmesan cheese
¾ pound natural Swiss cheese, grated
4 cups (1 quart) light cream (half-and-half)

1½ teaspoons salt
½ teaspoon sugar
¼ teaspoon (or more) freshly grated nutmeg
¼ teaspoon white pepper

The Garnish
2 tablespoons minced parsley (optional)

Preheat the oven to 375°. Form the pastry into a rectangle and roll out on a floured surface to measure about 18x15 inches. Roll or wrap the dough around the rolling pin and transfer to a 15½x10½x1-inch jelly roll pan. Do not skimp on the size of the pan or you will have too much filling. (We use a pan with a white nonstick lining.)

Trim the excess pastry, form a rim and flute the edges with your fingers or the handle of a wooden spoon. (To prevent shrinkage, you can place the pan in the freezer at this point for at least 15 minutes.) Now line the inside of the pan with a strip of foil large enough to cover the dough. Fill with beans. Bake for 20 minutes. The partial baking helps keep the crust from getting soggy. Set aside to cool while you prepare the filling.

In a large skillet cook the bacon until crisp. Drain on paper towels, then crumble finely. If you like a pronounced bacon flavor, pour out all but 2 tablespoons of the bacon drippings from the skillet. For a milder flavor, pour out all the drippings and stir in 2 tablespoons of butter or margarine. When melted, sauté the minced onion until lightly browned. Set aside.

Separate one egg and place the yolk in a large mixing bowl and the white in a small bowl. Beat the white until frothy and brush it over the inside of the pastry shell to further "waterproof" the pastry. Sprinkle the Parmesan evenly over the bottom of the shell, followed by an even sprinkling of Swiss cheese. Top with the bacon.

Now to the reserved egg yolk, add the remaining eggs, half-and-half, seasonings, beating until well combined. Stir in the sautéed onion. Carefully pour the mixture over the ingredients in the pastry shell. Bake the quiche in the center of the oven for about 45 minutes or until the top is browned and the center feels firm when gently pressed with your finger. Cool on a rack for at least 10 minutes before cutting.

To serve, cut the quiche into 50 to 60 squares, depending on how large you want the pieces to be. Sprinkle lightly with parsley and transfer to a warm plate for serving.

To Prepare in Advance. Up to 12 hours in advance, bake the quiche and leave it at room temperature. Cut and serve at room temperature. Or, reheat the squares on a cookie sheet at 325° to 375° for 5 to 7 minutes. We do not recommend refrigerating or freezing the quiche after baking; it will affect the creamy texture.

COOKED ARTICHOKES

    1 large artichoke
    1 tablespoon lemon juice
    1 tablespoon olive oil
    1 clove garlic, bruised but left whole

For 16 Servings. Cook two artichokes; do not increase other ingredients.

For 32 Servings. Three artichokes should be sufficient; do not increase other ingredients.

Trim the base of the artichoke flush and flat. With scissors, trim ¼ inch off the points of each leaf. For at least 30 minutes, soak the artichoke in cold salted water to cover, weighted down with a plate. Bugs lurking in the leaves will die and float to the surface. Rinse the artichoke and place in a deep saucepan (not aluminum) with the lemon juice, olive oil, garlic, and sufficient water to cover. Simmer, covered, for 40 to 45 minutes, or until the bottom (heart) is tender when pierced with a fork.

Drain and cool. Spread the top leaves apart until you see the tiny tender leaves that cover the hairy choke. With a small spoon, scrape away the leaves and choke. Place a small glass or bowl in the hollow to hold the dip. Pull off a few of the outer leaves and place them sunflower fashion around the artichoke on a serving dish. Serve at room temperature. For large parties, make two or three and replace with a fresh artichoke and dip when the first one looks tired.

To Prepare in Advance. Cooked artichokes can be refrigerated in a plastic bag up to four days.

Afterthought. This is our favorite method for serving hot individual artichokes. Fill the center container with warm hollandaise or lemony Greek avgolemono sauce. Never cook just one artichoke; extras are always great to have on hand.

MARJORIE'S DIP
For 16 servings

    1 egg
    1 egg yolk
    About ½ cup well-packed parsley leaves (no stems)
    ¼ medium onion, chopped
    1 tablespoon freshly squeezed lemon juice
    1 tablespoon Dijon-style mustard (preferably Poupon label)
    1 tablespoon chopped fresh dill, or a pinch dried dill weed
    2 teaspoons chicken stock base (preferably Spice Islands label),
       or 1 teaspoon celery salt
    1½ tablespoons capers, drained
    1 teaspoon minced fresh sweet basil, or a pinch of dried sweet basil
    1 teaspoon minced fresh tarragon leaves, or a pinch dried tarragon
    ½ teaspoon freshly ground black pepper
    1 cup mild olive oil
    ¼ cup sour cream

Note: Sherry vinegar, available at specialty food stores, is our choice for use in dips and salad dressings. It is stronger than wine vinegar, so use it sparingly.

Place the egg and yolk in the container of an electric blender, or in a food processor fitted with a steel blade. Run the motor for a second or two. Add the remaining ingredients, except for the olive oil and sour cream. Blend a few seconds to purée the onion. With the motor running, pour in the olive oil in a very slow, steady stream. The mixture will have the consistency of thin mayonnaise. Add the sour cream and whirl just to mix. Serve the dip at room temperature.

To Prepare in Advance. The dip will keep in the refrigerator at least a week. Do not freeze. Bring to room temperature before serving.

Afterthought. This dip makes an excellent salad dressing that is reminiscent of a tangy Green Goddess without anchovies. If the dip is a bit too zesty for your palate, add some mayonnaise or sour cream to lighten the flavor. Adding the mayonnaise will not change the consistency, but sour cream will thin the dip slightly.

FRESHLY COOKED SHRIMP WITH PESTO DIP
2 pounds large or extra-large raw shrimp in their shells (see *Note*)

The Court Bouillon
2 quarts cold water
2 teaspoons salt
6 to 8 peppercorns
1 lemon, sliced
Sliced celery leaves, a bit of chopped onion, and a few parsley stems, as desired

To Serve
Pesto Dip (recipe follows)

For 16 Servings. Recipe may be doubled. Increase court bouillon by half.

For 32 Servings. A triple recipe should be sufficient. Double court bouillon for 6 pounds of shrimp.

Note: Buying raw frozen shrimp at a reputable fish market will give you the best quality and value. This may be contrary to everything you've heard, but shrimp are now usually "flash-frozen" right on the fishing boats. Even so-called "fresh shrimp" on sale have been frozen. The strong ammonia flavor and odor that develop come only with age and overcooking. Thaw frozen shrimp under cold running water and cook them as soon as possible. If you plan to keep them frozen for a period of time, keep your freezer at 0° or below.

Place the shrimp (thawed, if frozen) in a large pot or Dutch oven with the court bouillon ingredients. Bring to a simmer over medium-high heat, stirring once or twice. When the mixture starts boiling, remove the pan from the heat. Cool the shrimp in the court bouillon for 5 to 10 minutes; the time will depend on the size of the shrimp. Drain. Remove the shells. Make a small incision along the curve of the back with a small sharp knife and lift out the black vein with the point of the knife. Wash the shrimp under cold running water. Dry on paper towels and chill until serving time.

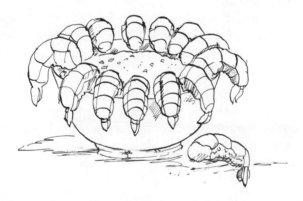

To Prepare in Advance. Naturally, the sooner served, the better. After cooking the shrimp, store in a plastic bag in the refrigerator up to three days. Do not freeze. An hour before guests arrive, arrange them on a serving platter with the Pesto Dip, cover with plastic wrap, and keep chilled.

PESTO DIP
¾ cup mayonnaise
¼ cup Pesto Genovese (see Recipes index)

For 32 Servings. A triple recipe should be sufficient.

Combine the mayonnaise and pesto. Serve, surrounded by the freshly cooked shrimp, in a seashell or small dish.

To Prepare in Advance. Mix the dip up to 48 hours before serving, cover, and refrigerate. Do not freeze.

KIELBASA IN DARK BEER WITH TARRAGON

1 pound kielbasa (Polish sausage)
1 (12-ounce) bottle Löwenbrau Dark Special beer
1½ teaspoons fresh tarragon, minced, or ½ teaspoon dried tarragon, crumbled

Slice the kielbasa in ½-inch-thick diagonal slices. Place in a saucepan with the beer and tarragon. Simmer slowly for 10 to 15 minutes. Cool the sausage, then refrigerate in the beer overnight.

Before serving, discard the congealed fat and reheat the beer and sausage to a simmer. Drain all the liquid, reserving the liquid if you want to poach more kielbasa. Place the slices on a warm platter and serve with frilled toothpicks.

To Prepare in Advance. It is imperative to poach the kielbasa at least 12 hours in advance. Store the slices in the poaching liquid and refrigerate up to one week. Reheat to serve. Poached kielbasa also freezes well and can be made prepared one month in advance.

ROUND RYE SANDWICH

About 32 wedge-shaped sandwiches for at least 16 servings

2-pound round loaf of fresh, seedless rye bread, homemade or baked to order from your local baker

The Sandwich Fillings

½ pound (2 sticks) butter, softened (see *Note*)
¼ pound rare roast beef, sliced paper thin

¼ pound baked ham, sliced paper thin
Freshly ground black pepper

The Garnish
Parsley flowerets and daisies or other fresh flowers

Note: Soft margarine may be substituted, but do not use mayonnaise or "diet" margarine (the latter has a high water content that will make the sandwiches soggy).

For 32 Servings. Make two 2-pound loaves; or make a large 4-pound loaf, double the filling ingredients, and make 6 layers of sandwiches cut in twelfths.

Slice off the top and the bottom of the loaf, and make matching notches so that you can fit the pieces together later. Cut the bread loose from the crust by running a serrated grapefruit knife all around the inside top edge. Repeat the process from the bottom of the loaf. This should give you a ½-inch-thick shell. (We use an inexpensive knife—available at most supermarkets—because it bends easily to fit the curves of the loaf.) Remove the crust shell and place it with the top and bottom slices in a plastic bag to prevent drying out while you make the sandwiches from the "core" of the bread.

Cut the core in half crosswise, stand each half on the crosswise cut, and cut each half lengthwise into nine even slices. Discard one slice from each half (this will leave eight slices in each half) to compensate for the room required by the fillings. Make four ham sandwiches from one half of the loaf and four roast beef sandwiches from the other half, completely coating the bread next to the meat with softened butter to prevent sogginess. Lightly salt the roast beef sandwiches; sprinkle both the beef and the ham with a generous amount of ground black pepper. Trim the meat even with the bread. Stack the sandwiches and reassemble the halves to form the original round. Use a serrated or electric carving knife to cut the round in eighths, making four layers of eight sandwiches. Remove the crust ring from the plastic bag and gently fit it over the outside of the sandwiches. Replace the top and bottom crusts. Remove one sandwich and eat it; for some unknown reason, most people are reluctant to take the first sandwich.

Serve the loaf on a round platter surrounded by parsley clusters and fresh flowers, if available, placed in water tubes to preserve freshness.

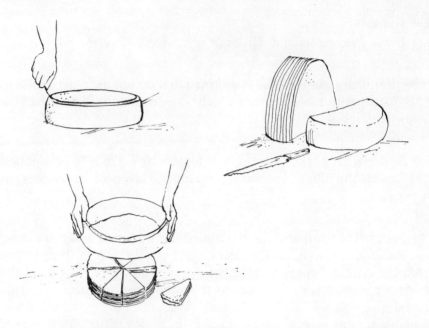

To Prepare in Advance. Wrap the fully prepared loaf in a damp tea towel and refrigerate in a plastic bag up to 48 hours. Redampen the towel as needed to prevent drying out. The loaf can also be prepared and frozen one month in advance.

Afterthought. We have experimented with other fillings. Tongue, Swiss cheese, thin-sliced turkey, and chicken are fine. Fish is not because the aroma will permeate the whole loaf.

PLATTER OF ASSORTED CHEESES AND CRACKERS

Few arrangements look more appetizing to us than an assortment of varied rounds and wedges of contrasting cheeses artfully displayed on a large wooden board.

There are very few rules that apply to the serving of cheese, but they are important. For fullest flavor, all cheeses are best served at room temperature. As much as possible and practical, retain the original shape of the cheese as you cut: Cut a wedge-shape serving from the side of a wedge; cut a slice from the end of a block. A large round is best served with a cheese scraper to curl a slice of cheese from the top. If you ruin the shape of a piece of cheese, grate it into another dish or salad.

To create your cheese tray, choose a variety of tastes, textures, shapes, and colors. A shop that specializes in cheese will be happy to advise you. Select a creamy Brie, a pungent bleu, a sharp Cheddar, and something unconventional, such as Banon, a French goat cheese wrapped in a chestnut leaf. Figure on approximately 4 ounces of cheese per guest. Dress up the tray with a tiny pot of parsley and fresh flowers if available. Accompany with an assortment of plain, unseasoned crackers to nibble with the cheese.

To Prepare in Advance. Place the cheeses on the serving board up to 6 hours before serving. Press plastic wrap onto all the cut surfaces to preserve freshness. Just before serving remove the wrap, add garnish and crackers, and serve.

CHAFING DISH CHILI WITH CONDIMENTS

    4 pounds lean beef (chuck or round)
    2 medium onions, minced
    2 tablespoons bacon drippings or butter
    3 medium cloves garlic, minced or pressed
    2½ cups well-seasoned beef broth (if canned, undiluted)
    1 (8-ounce) can tomato sauce
    ⅓ to ½ cup chili powder
    1 tablespoon ground cumin
    2 teaspoons dried oregano, crumbled
    2 teaspoons Worcestershire sauce
    2 tablespoons Quaker *masa harina* (tortilla flour) or Wondra
      instant-blending flour

1 (15-ounce) can pinto beans, drained
Salt to taste

Condiments

8 ounces Cheddar cheese, grated
8 ounces sour cream
6 scallions, including some of the green tops, thinly sliced

For 16 Servings. Recipe may be doubled, but add an extra tablespoon of *masa harina* or flour when thickening.

For 32 Servings. Not all your guests will indulge, so a double recipe should be sufficient.

Trim the meat of all fat and cut into ¼-inch dice. If you have a food processor, cut the meat in 1-inch cubes and coarsely grind about a pound at a time by turning the motor quickly on and off until the meat is chopped in small dice. Set the meat aside.

Sauté the onion in the bacon drippings or butter over medium heat until lightly browned. Stir in the garlic and cook it for a few seconds. Add the meat, mashing it constantly with the back of a spoon to break up any lumps; cook it for 5 to 7 minutes until all traces of pink disappear. Stir in 2 cups of the beef broth, the tomato sauce, chili powder, cumin, oregano, and Worcestershire sauce. Bring the mixture to a simmer, then reduce the heat and simmer slowly, uncovered, for 1 hour.

Stir in the *masa harina* or flour into the remaining ½ cup beef broth until smooth and slowly stir the mixture into the simmering chili. Blend well; cook slowly for about 10 minutes longer. Stir in the drained pinto beans and heat through. Taste for seasoning; add salt if needed.

Keep chili hot in a chafing dish placed over a water-bath. Or serve it in the removable crock of a crock-pot; it will stay hot for quite a long time. Place the condiments in individual bowls with serving spoons and set next to the chili. Provide your guests with small soufflé dishes or soup bowls for self-service.

To Prepare in Advance. The chili can be refrigerated five days or frozen up to four months. On the morning of your party, place the condiments in their serving bowls. Cover cheese and scallions with damp paper towels and keep chilled, along with the sour cream.

ENCORES

If you have a considerable amount of food left, why not plan a leftovers party? It can be very casual, requiring little extra work. Use up the quiche, kielbasa, and any perishable desserts as soon as possible. Trim and rewrap the cheeses for refrigerator storage. Use Marjorie's Dip for salad dressing. Freeze leftover sandwiches individually to serve when needed in lunch bags or with soup or salad. Chili makes a great supper or snack, served plain, or as a topping for hamburgers, hot dogs, or omelettes. Serve the artichokes warm with melted butter. The tarts should be eaten, but the other sweets should be frozen if not frozen earlier and the candy stored in airtight tins.

CHAMPAGNE-to-CASSOULET BUFFET

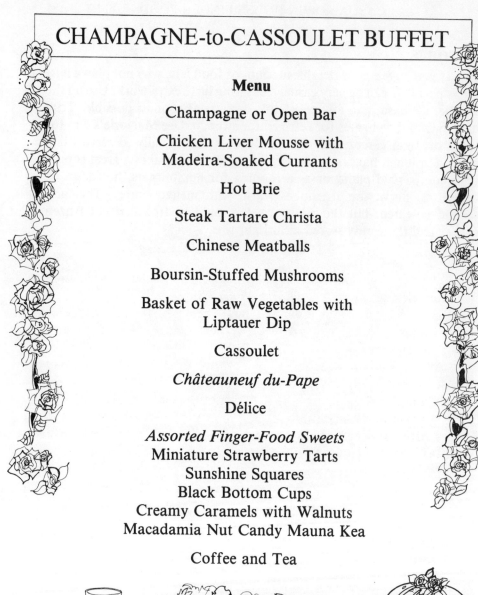

Menu

Champagne or Open Bar

Chicken Liver Mousse with
Madeira-Soaked Currants

Hot Brie

Steak Tartare Christa

Chinese Meatballs

Boursin-Stuffed Mushrooms

Basket of Raw Vegetables with
Liptauer Dip

Cassoulet

Châteauneuf du-Pape

Délice

Assorted Finger-Food Sweets
Miniature Strawberry Tarts
Sunshine Squares
Black Bottom Cups
Creamy Caramels with Walnuts
Macadamia Nut Candy Mauna Kea

Coffee and Tea

ELEGANT OPEN HOUSE, CHAMPAGNE-TO-CASSOULET BUFFET

For the occasions when a cocktail party requires a certain elegance, here's a menu that will both impress and satisfy your guests. We suggest hiring a bartender for the occasion and at least one other helper to assist in passing food at the beginning when everyone is getting acquainted.

All the foods do not need to be on the main buffet table. We make it a point to arrange neat groupings of attractive appetizers and sweets throughout the entertaining area to prevent the usual buffet table traffic jam. We also find it helpful to make duplicate platters of several of the dishes offered; when one looks untidy and unappetizing, it can be replaced with a fresh one from the kitchen.

The Hot Brie is a specialty of Sheila Ricci, who serves this dish at her Right Bank Tea Room on Rodeo Drive in Beverly Hills.

The recipe for Steak Tartare comes to us via our friends, Christa and Peter Zinner. It can also double as a main course—allow about ¼ pound of meat per person and accompany it with a Cabernet Sauvignon or mugs of icy cold beer.

We are grateful to Frances Pelham for the delicious meatballs and to our next-door neighbor, Mikki Olsen, for the dazzling array of raw vegetables in a basket. The Liptauer dip that accompanies the vegetables adheres to them very well. Guests appreciate the fact that it doesn't drip on them or on the carpet.

The rich Délice takes only minutes to make and is always great to have on hand in the freezer. The recipes for the finger-food sweets appear in the Exotic Curry and Chutney Buffet.

About ten o'clock we plan a change of pace and bring a hot and hearty Cassoulet, a provincial French dish, to the table. We time its serving to provide the guests with something substantial in their stomachs for the drive home.

THE TABLE SETTINGS

This is an elaborate, single-line buffet. Serving help will be required. Champagne or cocktails are served at the bar; desserts are served separately. The Cassoulet, for which forks and serving plates are required, replaces the meatballs later in the evening.

Centerpiece

Buffet Table. You will need a shallow, rectangular basket, an oval dish to fit inside the basket, several heads of Bibb lettuce, fresh flowers (roses, daisies, chrysanthemums, or whatever is seasonal), and water tubes (available from your florist). To give your arrangement height in the center, invert the dish in the middle of the basket. Cover the entire surface with lettuce. Insert the flowers in the water tubes and arrange on the lettuce, hiding the tubes among the leaves. Spray the arrangement with a mister to keep it fresh and moist. The centerpiece can be arranged the morning of the party, covered with a damp tea towel, and stored in a cool, dark place.

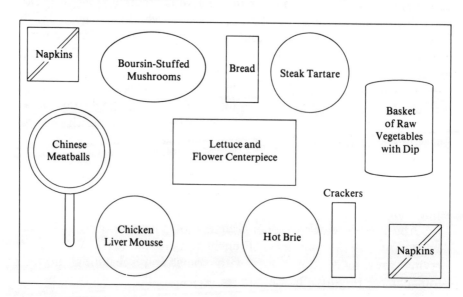

TIMETABLE

Several Weeks Before the Party. Because of the complexity of the menu, begin planning as early as possible. Hire a bartender. If champagne will be featured instead of hard liquor, arrange for tubs in which the bottles can be iced. Make the meatballs and the Cassoulet and freeze them. If you are serving an assortment of sweets, refer to the timetable for the Exotic Curry and Chutney Buffet and prepare and refrigerate or freeze the finger-food sweets involved. Make and refrigerate the Délice.

One Week Before the Party. Make the Liptauer Dip and the Délice. Marinate the currants in Madeira for the mousse.

Three Days Before the Party. Make the Chicken Liver Mousse. Do your marketing; make a special trip to a cheese shop for a perfectly ripened Brie. Toast the almonds for the Hot Brie.

Two Days Before the Party. Make the Cassoulet if you did not freeze it in advance. Make the sweet-and-sour sauce for the meatballs.

The Day Before the Party. Wash the lettuce and parsley and cut all the raw vegetables for the dip. Wrap in damp paper towels and refrigerate individually in plastic bags to stay fresh. Thaw the meatballs, the Cassoulet if frozen, and any frozen desserts.

The Morning of the Party. Mix the seasonings for the Steak Tartare and leave at room temperature. Place the Brie, topped with almonds, in its baking dish in the refrigerator. Stuff the mushrooms, sprinkling with parsley if they are to be served cold, or with paprika if they will be broiled. Refrigerate. Within 6 hours of serving, whip the cream for the dessert topping. Bring the Liptauer Dip to room temperature.

COUNTDOWN

1 hour before guests arrive:	Make Steak Tartare; chill serving dish. Bring Cassoulet to room temperature. Arrange and decorate Basket of Raw Vegetables with Dip.
45 minutes before guests arrive:	Check the bar setup, fill ice buckets; or ice the champagne. Arrange platter of assorted sweets, if serving.

	Open red wine to "breathe" and place in cool spot.
30 minutes before guests arrive:	Set out the mushrooms if serving them at room temperature
15 minutes before guests arrive:	Heat meatballs in sauce and transfer to chafing dish with water jacket. Prepare coffee and tea.
5 minutes before guests arrive:	Set out Steak Tartare with spreaders and bread. Set out Chicken Liver Mousse with spreaders and crackers.
After guests arrive:	Heat Brie at 475° until soft. Serve with crackers. Broil mushrooms if not serving them at room temperature. Heat Cassoulet for 45 minutes at 350°.
About an hour before guests depart:	Serve Cassoulet and red wine.

RECIPES

CHICKEN LIVER MOUSSE WITH MADEIRA-SOAKED CURRANTS

For 3 cups, or up to 32 servings

¼ cup dried currants
¼ cup Madeira
1 pound chicken livers
2 tablespoons butter
4 large shallots, minced (see *Note*)
1 small clove garlic, pressed
1 tablespoon (1 envelope) plain gelatin
½ cup rich chicken broth
1 teaspoon celery salt
¼ teaspoon dried thyme leaves, crumbled
¼ teaspoon freshly ground black pepper

¼ pound (1 stick) butter, at room temperature
½ cup heavy cream (whipping cream)

Note: If shallots are not available, purple onions or the white part of scallions are an acceptable substitute.

At least 24 hours before making the mousse, combine the Madeira with the currants in a small container. Cover tightly and set aside to plump.

To make the mousse, rinse the livers well under cold running water and dry with paper towels. Cut the livers in half. Melt the butter in a large heavy skillet. Stir in the shallots and garlic. Sauté for about a minute over medium heat. Do not brown the mixture. Add the chicken livers to the skillet and sauté until almost done, about 3 to 5 minutes. They should remain light pink in the centers.

Meanwhile, sprinkle the gelatin over the chicken broth and set aside to soften for 5 minutes. When the livers are cooked, transfer them to the container of an electric blender or a food processor fitted with a steel blade. Drain the Madeira from the currants; add it to the chicken liver mixture, reserving the currants. Add the softened gelatin, celery salt, thyme, and pepper. Blend until completely smooth. Transfer to a mixing bowl. Cool completely to room temperature before proceeding or the texture of the finished mousse will be oily.

When the mixture is thoroughly cooled, cut the butter into small pieces and beat it into the chicken liver mixture. Whip the cream until it holds a soft shape—do not overbeat it. Fold the cream into the mousse, followed by the reserved currants. Spoon the mousse lightly into a 3-cup crock or into two 1½-cup crocks. Smooth the top(s) and cover tightly with plastic wrap. Chill until serving time.

To Prepare in Advance. Store, tightly covered, in the refrigerator up to three days. The mousse does not freeze particularly well because the gelatin turns slightly rubbery.

HOT BRIE

1 pound round of perfectly ripened Brie (see *Note*)
¾ cup slivered blanched almonds, chopped
1 tablespoon butter

To Serve

Unseasoned crackers, such as Bremner wafers

Note: Perfectly ripened Brie is difficult to find. Buy it only from a reputable dealer whom you trust. The skin should have a delicate flavor, not a strong ammonia taste as it does when overripened.

For 32 Servings. A 2-pound round of Brie will be more than ample. Use 1½ cups of nuts and 2 tablespoons butter.

Preheat oven to 475°. Place the chilled Brie in a ceramic quiche dish or ovenproof serving dish that measures at least 2 inches larger in diameter than the cheese round. Heat the nuts with the butter in a small skillet until lightly toasted. Spread the nuts evenly over the top of the cheese. Bake at 475° until the cheese feels soft and starts to break the skin, about 4 to 7 minutes. The time will depend on the ripeness of the Brie and its temperature when it goes into the oven. Serve immediately with plain crackers and spreaders.

To Prepare in Advance. Several hours before serving, place the cheese in the baking dish. Brown the nuts and spread them over the cheese. Chill until time to bake. Then proceed as directed above.

Afterthought. The cheese can quickly be prepared in a microwave oven. Heat the plate first or the cheese will resolidify rapidly. The almonds can be toasted up to three days in advance. Store in a plastic bag or jar in the refrigerator.

STEAK TARTARE CHRISTA
   2 tablespoons minced onion
   1½ teaspoons vegetable oil or olive oil
   ¾ teaspoon minced tarragon or ¼ teaspoon dried tarragon, crumbled (optional)

½ teaspoon paprika
¾ pound lean beef (round steak or sirloin, not top sirloin), trimmed of all fat and connective tissue, cut into 1-inch chunks
1½ tablespoons Worcestershire sauce
½ jigger (¾ ounce) vodka or aquavit
1½ teaspoons Dijon-style mustard (preferably Poupon label)
1 egg yolk
¼ to ½ teaspoon salt
⅛ teaspoon freshly ground black pepper

To Serve
1 tablespoon minced parsley
1 tablespoon capers, drained and rinsed
Thin-sliced triangles of pumpernickel or rye bread, plain melba rounds, or any thin toast points
Small bowls of coarse salt (kosher salt) and cracked pepper

For 32 Servings. The recipe may be quadrupled. Fill a 6- to 8-cup mold or two 3- to 4-cup molds, refrigerating one for later use. We prefer the use of two molds for a large party because we can freshen the look of the table by replacing the first with the second halfway through the evening.

In a mixing bowl, combine the onion, oil, tarragon, and paprika. Let stand at room temperature for at least 30 minutes to allow the flavors to blend.

No more than 2 hours before serving, grind the meat. If you are using a food processor, place the meat in the bowl with the steel blade. Chop one cupful at a time, turning the motor on and off in four or five short bursts, until it is evenly chopped, finer than hamburger but not mushy or pasty. Combine the ground meat with the onion mixture and all remaining ingredients. Taste for seasoning and adjust with salt and pepper to your liking.

Spray the inside of a 1½- to 2-cup mold with nonstick cooking spray, followed by an even sprinkling of minced parsley. Press the steak tartare firmly into the mold, then turn out onto a chilled serving plate. Stud with capers. Surround with bread, melba rounds, or toast, and supply small spreaders for serving. Guests may sprinkle the steak tartare with salt and pepper, if desired.

To Prepare in Advance. For maximum freshness, prepare and chill within 2 hours of serving.

CHINESE MEATBALLS
For 16 servings

The Meatballs
    1 pound lean ground beef
    1 cup chopped or slivered blanched almonds
    ¾ cup finely minced celery
    2 eggs, slightly beaten
    1 clove garlic, pressed
    ½ cup soft bread crumbs (see *Note*)
    1 tablespoon soy sauce
    1 teaspoon salt
    About ½ cup cornstarch to coat the meatballs
    Vegetable oil for frying

The Sweet-and-Sour Sauce
    2 cups rich chicken broth
    1 cup sugar
    1 cup white wine vinegar (preferably Regina label)
    1 (1-pound) can pineapple chunks, packed in juice
    2 to 4 ounces canned pineapple juice, as needed
    6 tablespoons cornstarch
    4 tablespoons soy sauce
    1 green pepper, cut in ½-inch cubes

Note: Soft bread crumbs are easy to make in a blender or food processor from fresh or day-old bread.

For 32 Servings. Make a double quantity of the meatballs, but only 1½ times as much sauce.

Mix the meatball ingredients thoroughly, using your hands or the paddle attachment of an electric mixer. Form into forty 1-inch small balls, roll in cornstarch to coat. Fry in salad oil until browned and cooked through, or bake 1 inch apart in a shallow pan at 400° for 20 to 30 minutes until done.

To make the sauce, combine the broth, sugar, and vinegar in a heavy pot and bring to a simmer. Drain the pineapple chunks, reserving the juice. Add canned pineapple juice to the reserved juice to make 1 cup. Add the cornstarch to the pineapple juice, stirring until smooth. Pour the pineapple juice and soy sauce into the simmering mixture.

Cook and stir until thickened. Remove from heat. Before serving, add the meatballs, pineapple chunks, and green pepper to the sauce and heat gently. Serve in a chafing dish to keep warm. Provide cocktail picks or small forks for guests to help themselves.

To Prepare in Advance. The meatballs can be refrigerated up to four days. Make the sauce up to two days ahead and refrigerate. Combine as described above and heat gently until the meatballs are heated through. Overheating cornstarch-thickened sauces causes them to thin out. The meatballs and sauce can also be made up to three months in advance and frozen separately.

BOURSIN-STUFFED MUSHROOMS
For 16 servings

> 20 to 24 medium-size fresh mushrooms
> 1 tablespoon vegetable oil
> 1 (5-ounce) package garlic-and-herb-flavored Boursin cheese, softened
> Minced parsley (if serving cold), or paprika (if serving hot)

Wash the mushrooms under cold running water, holding them stems down and rubbing your fingers over the surface of the cap to remove any dirt. Do this quickly so that the mushrooms do not absorb any water. Dry immediately on paper towels. Twist out the stems and reserve them for another use. Lightly rub the oil on the outside of the caps to prevent drying. Fill each cavity with cheese, pressing it in firmly and mounding slightly.

To serve at room temperature, sprinkle the cheese with minced parsley and arrange the mushrooms on a serving dish. Cover loosely with a damp paper towel until serving time.

To serve hot, preheat your broiler. Arrange the mushrooms close together on a pan that will fit under the broiler. Sprinkle paprika lightly over the cheese for color. Broil about 4 inches from the heat until the cheese begins to bubble. Cool slightly so that the mushrooms can be comfortably picked up with the fingers. Serve immediately.

To Prepare in Advance. The mushrooms can be filled with cheese 24 hours before serving. Cover with damp paper towels and refrigerate. If serving at room temperature, remove from the refrigerator 1 hour before serving and garnish with parsley.

Afterthought. Liptauer Dip also makes a delicious filling for raw mushrooms; serve at room temperature.

BASKET OF RAW VEGETABLES WITH LIPTAUER DIP
For 8 to 32 servings

A large, shallow basket with a handle
6 to 8 red and green peppers to hold the raw vegetables
2 heads salad bowl lettuce or other variety to line the basket
A large shell or bowl to hold the Liptauer Dip (recipe follows)
1 bunch small carrots with leafy green tops to decorate the handle
1 bunch parsley
String or twister seals
1 yard wide ribbon for a bow

Raw Vegetables (amount depends on how large a variety you choose)
Raw zucchini spears
Asparagus spears, scraped with a peeler to remove tough outer flesh
Scallions
Carrot spears
Celery spears
Belgian endive, cut in quarters through the stem
Cherry tomatoes
Mushrooms, cut in quarters through the stem
Radishes
Caulifloweretes

To prepare the basket, cut the tops off the bell peppers and thin slices off the bottoms so that they will stand up. Remove the seeds and ribs and fill each pepper with an assortment of the raw vegetables. Line the basket with crisp fresh lettuce leaves and arrange the peppers filled with vegetables on top. On one side add the shell or bowl containing the Liptauer Dip; surround it with the remaining cut vegetables. Cherry tomatoes and mushrooms should be speared with toothpicks to make them easy to handle.

Decorate the top of the basket by using string or twister seals to fasten a bunch of carrots with leafy tops to the handle. Cover the string or seals with small bunches of parsley; tie in place with a ribbon bow.

To Prepare in Advance. Wrap the cut vegetables in damp paper towels and refrigerate in plastic bags up to 24 hours.

LIPTAUER DIP
For 3 cups, or 16 servings

1 (8-ounce) package cream cheese, at room temperature
¼ pound (1 stick) butter or margarine, at room temperature
1 cup (½ pint) large-curd cottage cheese
¼ cup scallions, thinly sliced, or 3 medium shallots, minced
1½ tablespoons caraway seeds
1½ tablespoons capers, drained
1 tablespoon paprika (see *Note*)
1 teaspoon Worcestershire sauce
1 teaspoon dry mustard
1 teaspoon salt
½ teaspoon freshly ground black pepper
1 medium clove garlic, pressed
½ cup sour cream

Note: Hungarian paprika is considered to be the finest. Store paprika (as well as cayenne and chili powder) in the refrigerator to prevent the appearance of small bugs.

For 32 Servings. How many servings there are to 3 cups of dip depends on the number of alternate hors d'oeuvres you will be serving. Double the recipe if your mixer is large enough, or simply make two batches.

In the large bowl of an electric mixer, combine the cream cheese and butter. Beat until very fluffy. Add all the remaining ingredients, except the sour cream. Beat about 5 minutes, stopping the motor from time to time to scrape down the sides of the bowl with a rubber spatula. Beat in the sour cream. Transfer to a bowl, cover, and let mellow in the refrigerator for at least 8 hours. Serve at room temperature.

To Prepare in Advance. The dip will keep at least one week in the refrigerator. Do not freeze.

CASSOULET
For 32 cocktail party servings, or 12 main-course servings

The Bean Mixture
4 cups (2 pounds) dried, small white beans or Great Northern beans
6 cups water
½ pound salt pork, cut in ½-inch cubes
1 large onion, minced
1 clove garlic, pressed
5 teaspoons salt
1 (1-pound) fully cooked sausage (preferably kielbasa)

The Meat Sauce Mixture
1 pound boneless lamb from shoulder or leg
1½ pounds boneless pork loin
¼ cup rendered goose or duck fat, or 2 tablespoons *each* butter and vegetable oil
2 medium onions, minced
6 cloves garlic, pressed
8 cups dry white table wine
2 pounds fresh tomatoes, peeled, or 1 (1-pound 12-ounce) can Italian-style tomatoes
1 tablespoon tomato paste
1¼ teaspoons dried thyme, crumbled

The Topping
12 tablespoons (1½ sticks) butter
3 cups fresh bread crumbs
1 cup minced parsley

Rinse and pick over the beans. If you have enough time, soak the beans overnight in cold water to cover. If you are in a hurry, cover the beans with boiling water to a depth of 1 inch and soak for 1 hour. Drain and rinse the beans. Place them in a large kettle or Dutch oven with the water, salt pork, onions, and garlic. Simmer slowly for about 1½ hours or until the beans are almost tender. Stir in the salt and place the whole sausage on top. Simmer slowly until the beans are tender. Set aside.

Meanwhile, cut the lamb and pork in ½-inch cubes. In a large skillet, sauté the meat in the fat until it is lightly browned. Add the onion and garlic and cook about 5 minutes over medium heat until the onion is transparent. Stir in the wine, tomatoes and their liquid, tomato paste, and thyme. Break up the whole tomatoes by mashing them against the side of the pot with the edge of a spoon. Simmer slowly for 1 hour, uncovered, until the meat is very tender. Using a slotted spoon, transfer the meat to a bowl. Set aside. Boil the remaining sauce in the pot over high heat until it is reduced to 3 cups. Return the meat to the sauce.

Preheat the oven to 350°. You are now ready to assemble the Cassoulet. Use a 3-quart paella pan or earthenware casserole, or two smaller dishes. Make a 1-inch layer of beans (along with their cooking liquid) in the serving dish; top with some of the meat-sauce mixture. Repeat, making three or four layers of beans and sauce, ending with the sauce. How much of the beans and sauce you use for each layer will depend on how many dishes you are using to cook the Cassoulet. If you are using only one large casserole, use about one fourth of each for each layer. Slice the sausage diagonally and arrange it decoratively over the top.

Melt the butter for the topping in a medium skillet. Stir in the fresh bread crumbs to absorb the butter, then toss with the parsley. Evenly spread half this mixture over the top of the Cassoulet. Bake for about 20 minutes. Press the crumb topping down into the liquid with the back of a cooking spoon and top with the remaining crumb mixture. Bake 20 minutes longer or until the crumbs are browned.

To Prepare in Advance. For best flavor cook this dish at least one day ahead. Cool at room temperature, then cover, and refrigerate up to three days or freeze up to two months. Thaw if frozen and reheat before serving.

Afterthought. If you serve this as a main course, accompany it with a full-bodied red wine, such as a Chateâneuf de-Pape.

DÉLICE
For 16 servings

8 squares (8 ounces) unsweetened chocolate
½ pound (2 sticks) butter, at room temperature
1 (15-ounce) can unsweetened chestnut puree
1 cup sugar
2 teaspoons vanilla extract
3 tablespoons dark Jamaican rum (preferably Myer's label)
⅔ cup slivered blanched almonds, toasted

To Serve
Powdered sugar
3 roses with a little greenery, or several sprigs of holly (optional)
1 cup heavy cream (whipping cream), ⅓ cup powdered sugar, and
    1 teaspoon vanilla extract (optional)

Oil or spray with nonstick cooking spray a 5- or 6-cup ring mold or
an 8½ x 3⅝ x 2⅝-inch loaf pan. Melt the chocolate in the top of a double boiler placed over gently boiling water or in a microwave oven
according to manufacturer's directions. Set aside to cool.

In the large bowl of an electric mixer, cream the butter until light
and fluffy. Beat in the chestnut puree, a little at a time, until the mixture
is very creamy. Gradually beat in the sugar, followed by the cooled
chocolate, vanilla, and rum. Fold in the toasted almonds and turn the
mixture into the prepared mold. Pack it firmly, banging the mold on a
towel-covered counter to settle the mixture and prevent air pockets.
Chill at least 8 hours.

Unmold onto a doily-lined serving platter. Press powdered sugar
through a kitchen sieve with the back of a spoon and heavily dust over
the top of the dessert. Place roses with greenery or holly in a small cup
or vase in the center of the ring mold, or, if you use a loaf-shaped mold,
on the side of the serving plate.

Serve in *very thin* slices topped with sweetened whipped cream,
if desired. (Whip the cream until thickened; add the powdered
sugar—pressed through a kitchen sieve to remove lumps—and vanilla
extract and continue beating until peaks hold their shape when the
beater is lifted.)

To Prepare in Advance. Tightly wrapped in plastic wrap and then with
foil, this dessert can be stored up to two weeks in the refrigerator. It can
be frozen up to three months.

ENCORES

The Brie, Chicken Liver Mousse, mushrooms, and perishable finger-food sweets won't last long, so finish them as soon as possible. If the meatballs have been frozen before the party, go ahead and use them up. Otherwise freeze the meatballs and extra sauce separately. Make hamburgers with the leftover Steak Tartare. Soak raw cut vegetables in an ice-water bath to recrisp and serve the next day with any leftover dip. If there is a considerable amount of vegetables, consider making a hearty soup. The Cassoulet will last through several days of successive reheating. Soften the leftover Délice and press it into a smaller mold to serve again on another festive occasion. It may even be refrozen if you don't use it up.

Chili and Chowder Buffet

Menu

Beer or Wine

Crocked Cheese

Chafing Dish Chili
and
Hearty Clam Chowder

Buffet Salad Bowl

Elegant Hot Gingerbread

Coffee and Tea

WINTER'S EVE CHILI AND CHOWDER BUFFET

Here is the easiest buffet of all to serve, a true foul-weather friend. Ideal for after-the-game dining, for Halloween, New Year's — you name it.

The simplicity of these two dishes is deceptive. Humble as they seem, they are tasty and satisfying.

The Crocked Cheese is a no-fuss appetizer. The chili and chowder are simple to make in advance (in fact, the chili will improve in flavor) and can be reheated in two crock pots or chafing dishes, then served with a large bowl of salad greens with dressing on the side.

The chili is Texas-style chili. We profaned it slightly by adding a small amount of tomato sauce for taste and smoothness. The recipe appears in the Casual Open House, Finger-Food Buffet. The addition of small shell pasta to the clam chowder makes a hearty chowder, perfect for blustery days. If you prefer a more traditional chowder, omit the pasta.

Frances Pelham's Elegant Hot Gingerbread is the lightest, most delicate, and most delicious version we know. It will fill your home with an irresistible spicy fragrance while it bakes.

THE TABLE SETTINGS

This is an informal, double-line buffet. Fork and spoon are required. Appetizer, dessert, and beverages are served separately.

203

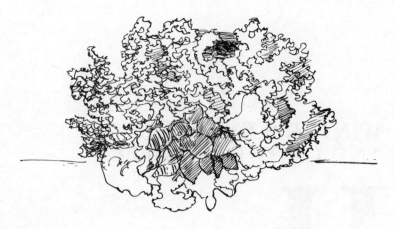

Centerpieces

Buffet Table. Lettuce and cherry tomatoes. You will need a round basket, several heads of salad bowl or butter lettuce, and cherry tomatoes with their stems intact. Cut off about 1 inch from the stem end of each head of lettuce. Fluff the leaves slightly and stand the heads in the basket. Spray with nonstick cooking spray and arrange tomatoes on the folds. Spray with a plant mister to keep moist. Store in the lower part of refrigerator up to six hours.

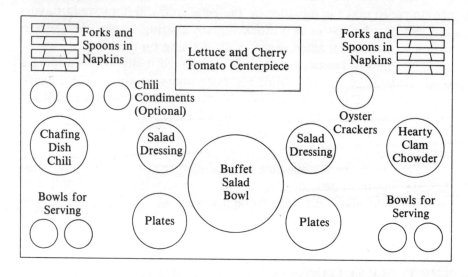

Dining Tables. Lettuce and radishes. For each centerpiece you will need a round basket, 1 head of red leaf lettuce, 1 head of salad bowl lettuce, and 1 bunch of radishes. Arrange leaves of red leaf lettuce around the rim of the basket. Cut 2 inches from the base of the salad bowl lettuce, stand it upright in the center, and open to hold the radishes, stems down. Spray the radishes with nonstick cooking spray to make them glisten and with a plant mister to keep them moist. Store, covered with a damp tea towel, up to six hours in the lower part of the refrigerator.

TIMETABLE

Five Days Before the Party. Make the chili for refrigerator storage. (Or, if you wish to freeze the chili, you may prepare it up to four months in advance.) Salad dressings may also be made and refrigerated. Prepare the Crocked Cheese without the garnish, seal with plastic wrap, and refrigerate.

The Day Before the Party. Make the chowder. Wash the salad greens and refrigerate.

The Day of the Party. Prepare the salad condiments, cover with a damp paper towel, and refrigerate. Chill the wine or beer. If you bake the gingerbread just before serving, set out the wet and dry ingredients separately in the morning. Whip the cream and chop the crystallized ginger for the gingerbread. Bring all dressings to room temperature. Prepare the centerpieces.

COUNTDOWN

30 minutes before guests arrive: Garnish the Crocked Cheese and set out with crackers.

Put beer and wine on ice for self-service.

Heat chili and chowder on "low" in crock pots or put on stove ready to reheat.

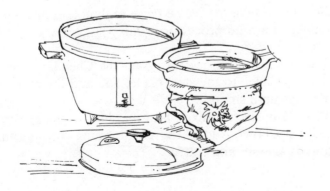

15 minutes before guests arrive:	Bake gingerbread.
	Whip cream for gingerbread and chill.
	Put dressing(s) on buffet table. Prepare coffee and tea.
10 minutes before serving:	Assemble salad and place on buffet.
	Reheat chili and chowder in crock pots if not already hot.
	Stir butter and parsley into chowder.
	Set out chili and chowder.
	Announce dinner.

RECIPES

CROCKED CHEESE
For 4 to 5 cups

½ pound sharp Cheddar cheese, finely grated, at room temperature
1 (8-ounce) package cream cheese
6 ounces Roquefort cheese (blue cheese may be substituted)
2 tablespoons butter or margarine, at room temperature
2 dashes Worcestershire sauce
Dash Tabasco sauce or pinch cayenne pepper
2 tablespoons cognac or brandy

To Serve

Chopped parsley or your choice of nuts
Small crackers, such as Wheat Thins

For 32 Servings. Make the recipe twice (a double recipe would be too large to make in a food processor or mixer).

If you use a food processor, grate the Cheddar cheese with the grating blade, change to the steel blade, and add the remaining ingredients. Process until smooth.

If you use an electric mixer, beat the cheeses together until smooth in a medium-size bowl. Add all the remaining ingredients and beat until the mixture is smooth and fluffy.

Pack the cheese mixture into crocks or other serving dishes. Seal tightly with plastic wrap and store in the refrigerator. Before serving, sprinkle the top of the cheese with chopped parsley or nuts for decoration.

To Prepare in Advance. It is important to let the spread mellow for at least three days before serving. If sealed airtight, it will keep up to one month in the refrigerator. Do not freeze.

HEARTY CLAM CHOWDER
For 8 servings

> 2 quarts live clams, scrubbed and washed (See *Note* in Red Clam Sauce recipe) or 2 (8-ounce) cans minced clams
> 1 (10-ounce) can whole baby clams
> ¼ pound salt pork, finely diced
> 2 medium onions, minced
> 1 medium red or green pepper, finely diced
> 2 tablespoons flour
> 2 teaspoons celery salt
> ¼ teaspoon freshly ground black pepper
> ¼ teaspoon dried summer savory, crumbled
> ¼ teaspoon dried thyme, crumbled
> 2 cups milk
> 1½ cups light cream (half-and-half)
> 2 dashes Worcestershire sauce
> 2 large potatoes, finely diced
> 2 cups small shell pasta
> Salt to taste

To Serve

> 1 tablespoon butter
> 2 tablespoons chopped parsley
> Oyster crackers

To steam the clams, place them in a kettle, add cold, lightly salted water (or part water and part white wine) to about ½-inch depth. This water will become the broth. Cover the pot and place over medium-high heat. Without lifting the lid, steam the clams for at least 8 minutes. Then check to see if all the clams have opened. If not, steam a few minutes longer. Discard the unopened clams. Lift the clams from the broth with a slotted spoon and set aside. Boil the broth over high heat until reduced to 1 cup of concentrated liquid. When the clams are cool enough to handle, remove them from their shells, mince and set aside. Discard the shells. If you are using canned minced clams, drain and reserve the juice. Do the same with the canned whole clams.

Use a heavy-bottomed pot (thick soups such as chowder scorch easily) and sauté the diced salt pork over medium heat until the fat is rendered and the pork is slightly crisp. Add the onions and bell pepper and sauté until transparent. Meanwhile, in a small bowl combine the flour, celery salt, pepper, summer savory, and thyme. When the onions are transparent, stir in the flour and seasonings mixture and cook for a few seconds. Stir in the milk, light cream, reserved clam broth, Worcestershire sauce, and potatoes. Bring the soup to a simmer over medium heat, reduce the heat, and continue to simmer until the potatoes are tender when tested. While the soup cooks, place the shell pasta in boiling salted water and cook until done; drain. When the potatoes are tender, stir in the minced and whole clams, pasta, and salt to taste — about a teaspoonful, depending on the saltiness of the clams. Do *not* cook the chowder after you add the clams or they will toughen.

Just before serving, stir in the butter and chopped parsley. Serve hot accompanied with oyster crackers.

To Prepare in Advance. The chowder will keep for one or two days in the refrigerator. Reheat it very gently to avoid toughening the clams. To serve, stir in the butter and chopped parsley.

BUFFET SALAD BOWL
For 16 servings

    2 heads Boston or Bibb lettuce
    1 head red leaf lettuce
    1 head salad bowl lettuce
    1 head romaine lettuce

The Condiments
    ½ pound fresh mushrooms, sliced ¼-inch thick through the stems
    1 bunch scallions, thinly sliced, including some of the green tops
    4 to 6 radishes, thinly sliced
    1 box cherry tomatoes, stemmed and cut in half

The Dressing
>3 cups Sherry Cream Dressing, or dressing of your choice
>(See 40-Ingredient Salad Bar Buffet)

For 32 Servings. Double the ingredients and store as directed in plastic bags. Replenish the buffet salad as needed from the reserved bags.

Wash all the greens and drain them well. Tear in bite-size pieces, wrap in paper towels, and place in sealed plastic bags for refrigerator storage.

Several hours before serving, place all the condiments in the bottom of your salad bowl (slice the mushrooms, but reassemble them in their original shape to keep them fresh) and place the mixed salad greens on top. Cover the greens with damp paper towels and store in the refrigerator until ready to serve.

Toss the greens and condiments together just before placing on the buffet table. Serve the dressing on the side.

To Prepare in Advance. The greens will stay crisp and fresh up to four days in the refrigerator, if washed and sealed in storage bags as directed. Prepare the condiments the morning of the party. Sherry Cream Dressing will keep in the refrigerator up to three weeks, but for best flavor bring to room temperature before serving.

ELEGANT HOT GINGERBREAD

3 large eggs
1 cup sugar
1 cup molasses
1 cup vegetable oil
1 teaspoon ground cloves
1 teaspoon ground ginger
1 teaspoon ground cinnamon
2 teaspoons baking soda
2 tablespoons hot water
2 cups sifted all-purpose flour
1 cup boiling water

To Serve

¾ cup heavy cream (whipping cream), ¼ cup powdered sugar, and ¾ teaspoon vanilla extract
1 tablespoon minced crystallized ginger

For 32 Servings. Make two double recipes in two separate batches.

Grease a 9x9x2-inch pan or an 11¾x7½x1¾-inch pan with shortening. Preheat the oven to 350°.

In a large mixing bowl beat together the eggs, sugar, molasses, and oil. Sift together the flour and spices. Dissolve the baking soda in the 2 tablespoons hot water and add to the wet ingredients. Gradually stir in the dry ingredients until well combined. Add the 1 cup boiling water; beat lightly and quickly and pour into the prepared pan. The batter will seem very thin. Bake for 45 minutes. Cool on a rack at least 15 minutes.

To serve, cut the warm gingerbread into squares or rectangles. Whip the cream until thickened; add the powdered sugar (pressed through a kitchen sieve to remove lumps) and vanilla extract and continue to whip until peaks hold their shape when the beater is lifted. Top each serving with a generous dollop of the whipped cream and a sprinkling of crystallized ginger. The whipped cream may also be combined with the ginger and set out in a serving bowl for guests to help themselves.

To Prepare in Advance. Gingerbread is at its best when freshly baked and still warm from the oven, but it may be made in advance and reheated, covered with foil, in a 300° oven for 10 minutes.

ENCORES

Any leftover chili may be frozen. The chowder contains potatoes, so it will not freeze well and should be eaten as soon as possible. If in doubt, toss it out. If any salad remains, discard the mushroom slices. Refrigerate the greens, wrap in a damp paper towel to recrisp, and refrigerate in a plastic bag for next-day serving. Leftover dressing will keep for a week in the refrigerator.

Gingerbread (this one at least) does not keep well. Do not refrigerate or freeze. Reheat in a regular oven wrapped in foil, or, for an instant snack, heat the gingerbread on a paper plate in a microwave oven.

APPENDIX

GARNISHES

"Whatever we look at with delight, whatever we see that gives us pleasure, though we may think we have forgotten it the next day, will influence us all of our lives." *George Santayana*

Garnishing food is an art that enhances the appearance of food and gives immediate pleasure to the senses of the observer and diner. If at first we eat with our eyes, as indeed we do, we are attracted to foods for their eye appeal. And although your delicate garnishes will be consumed and gone forever, your artistry will have impressed all who have shared your creative hospitality. In addition, garnishing a plate before a guest picks it up can keep the plate looking artistic and appealing no matter which foods are selected and combined—enhancing the appetite and continually pleasing the eye.

Every platter or plate of food is a picture, framed by the edge of the plate. Within that frame, your two most important decorative considerations are *height* and *color*. Many foods look two-dimensional on the plate, so you can use garnishes to add height—a three-dimensional contrast that is usually missing. Also give serious thought to the colors of the foods in your menu. Varied colors will perk up the appearance of the food, adding life and excitment to your party.

FRESH FLOWERS

From experience, we have found that white plates provide the freshest and most complementary background for any food. We also delight in the use of fresh flowers directly on the dinner plate. They add unusual and attractive designs, colors, and textures when used sparingly. In designing a flower garnish, never place an exposed flower stem into anything that is edible. We're not trying to discourage or frighten you but merely make you aware that out of the 300,000 known species of plants in the world, 500 are poisonous in varying degrees, for example, pink or white oleander blossoms and yellow jasmine. The chances of your selecting a toxic flower are remote, but if there's any doubt in your mind consult your local florist or library.

To eliminate the risk of toxicity, use miniature florist water tubes, small dark green plastic vials with rubber caps that sell for only a few cents apiece. They easily hold a small arrangement and can be hidden behind parsley, tucked under a lettuce leaf, or safely buried directly in some foods. If these water tubes are not available from your florist, take your fresh daisies, baby's breath, or vanda orchids and dip their stems in melted paraffin before use.

The rest of this chapter describes and illustrates how you can make garnishes that we have either created or adapted for our use.

PASTRY LEAVES AND FLOWERS

Attractive garnishes to add height and dimension to pies, tarts, tortes, and other pastries.

Pliers
2-inch biscuit cutter
Pastry dough
Rolling pin
Dinner fork
Wine bottle corks
Cookie sheets
1 egg, lightly beaten
Pastry brush
2-inch daisy cutter
Miniature muffin tins
Pastry tube nozzle

For Pastry Leaves. With the pliers, shape the biscuit cutter into a leaf (Figure 1).

On a floured surface, roll out the dough ⅛-inch thick and, using the cutter, cut as many leaves as you will need.

Hold the dinner fork lengthwise and lightly press the edge into the center of each leaf to make a long, thin, curved line from tip to stem. Now hold the fork flat and, starting from the top of the leaf and working toward the stem, press the points of the tines at an angle into the pastry on one side of the curved center line. Do not press too hard. You do not want to cut through the pastry dough. Repeat this "veining" process on the other side of the line (Figure 2). Set aside. Proceed similarly for all the leaves.

Cut the corks in half lengthwise. Start from the center of each half cork and shave away part of the cork in the shape of a wedge. Prepare

½ a cork for each leaf. Place the corks on a cookie sheet and drape a pastry leaf over each wedge (Figure 3).

Bake the leaves in a 375° oven 7 to 10 minutes until hard. Remove from the oven. Quickly brush the top of each leaf with the lightly beaten egg and return to the oven for a few minutes to turn the leaves a golden brown. Remove from oven; cool on the cookie sheet.

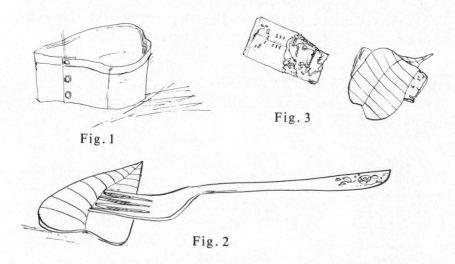

Fig. 3

Fig. 1

Fig. 2

For Pastry Flowers. On a floured surface roll out the dough ⅛-inch thick and, using the daisy cutter, cut as many daisies as you will need. Place each daisy in a lightly oiled miniature muffin tin. The diameter of the muffin cup should be smaller than the daisy so that when the flower is placed in the cup its petals are forced upward. With the large end (about ¾-inch wide) of a pastry tube nozzle, cut a circle for each daisy from the pastry. Place the circles on a cookie sheet.

Bake the daisies and circles at 375° about 7 to 10 minutes. When firm but not completely baked, remove from the oven. Paint the daisies generously but gently with the beaten egg. Remove the small circles from the cookie sheet and place one in the center of each flower.

Make certain to use sufficient egg glaze to "glue" the center piece firmly in place. Return to the oven and bake until the daisies are hard and turn a golden brown. Remove from the oven; cool. Gently remove from the muffin tins.

To decorate any crust, just "glue" in place with a liberal amount of egg wash 5 to 10 minutes before the dish is fully cooked. Finish baking with leaves and/or flowers in place. Or, use as is on top of any tart filling.

To Prepare in Advance. The leaves and flowers can be made ahead and kept at room temperature in a container up to one week, or frozen up to three months, wrapped in a paper towel and sealed in an airtight plastic bag. Corks can be reused indefinitely.

LONG-STEMMED STRAWBERRIES

When strawberries are stemless, add your own stems. Use as a garnish for the strawberry soufflé or serve as is.

Large strawberries, washed
Toothpick or skewer
Teaspoon
Melted chocolate
Parsley stems, cut into 3½-inch pieces

With the toothpick, make a hole in the stem end of each strawberry. With a teaspoon, place a drop or two of melted chocolate into the hole. Dip the thick end of the parsley stem into the melted chocolate and press it at least half an inch into the hole at the stem end. Place the finished strawberries on a platter and store in the refrigerator until the chocolate has hardened and you are ready to serve.

To Prepare in Advance. The strawberries can be prepared 24 hours in advance. Keep refrigerated.

MAGICAL MANGO

For 2 servings

Turn a mango inside out for easy eating.

1 ripe mango
8-inch chef's knife
Dull table knife
Fresh blueberries or raspberries
4 teaspoons grated coconut

Using the chef's knife, cut off a slice from the stem to the tip of each side of the mango, as close to the pit as you can. Discard the middle portion.

Hold one mango half, fruit side up, in the palm of one hand and, with the tip of the dull knife, make a series of deep diagonal cuts in the fruit (cut the meat but not the skin) in one direction, about ¾-inch apart. Repeat in the opposite direction to give a crisscross grid effect.

Now hold the scored mango half with both hands and push up from the middle of the skin side so that the grids open up. Repeat with the other half. Place each half on a serving dish, insert berries in the grid, top with coconut, and serve.

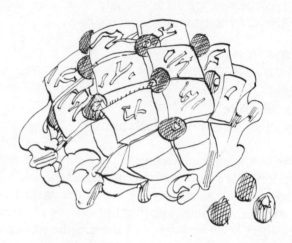

To Prepare in Advance. Mangoes are on the market from January until early September. Buy them firm, ripen at room temperature, and refrigerate until needed. Prepare the mangoes the day before, up to the point where they are cut in a design. Wrap individually in plastic wrap and refrigerate. When ready to serve, open up the grids, insert the berries, and top with coconut.

CARROT FLOWERS

A simple technique to transform carrot slices into flowers.

Carrots
Vegetable peeler
Mushroom fluter or lemon stripper
Sharp knife or mechanical slicer

With the vegetable peeler, peel the carrots under cold running water; remove stem and root ends. Place each carrot flat on a cutting board. Holding the thick end between the thumb and forefinger of your

left hand, use the mushroom fluter to cut a deep furrow down the entire length of the carrot. Rotate the carrot ⅛-inch and cut another furrow. Repeat around the entire carrot. Slice each carrot crosswise into ⅛-inch pieces. If a mechanical slicer is used, the shape of the flowers can vary from round to oval.

To Prepare in Advance. The carrot flowers can be prepared up to a week in advance, placed in a plastic bag with a damp paper towel, and refrigerated.

FLOWER GARNISH

A festive flower garnish for a buffet plate.

1 lemon
Sharp knife
Bamboo skewer
Parsley
3 daisies

Cut the lemon in half from stem to tip. Halve each half again from stem to tip. Cut each wedge in half. You should now have 8 small wedges.

With the knife, slit the skewer about 2 inches deep at the blunt end. Insert the stem of a small sprig of parsley into the slit. Spear the point end of the skewer through one side of the pulp and into the rind near one of the crescent ends of the lemon. As you pull it out from the opposite end, the parsley will stay imbedded in the lemon. Repeat this process on the other side with a parsley sprig and then in the center with a daisy. Cut the protruding stems flush with the lemon. Drop the finished lemon crescents in a pan of cold water until ready to use. Drain on paper towels before placing them on dinner plates.

To Prepare in Advance. The flower garnishes can be prepared the day before the party, placed in a pan of cold water, and refrigerated until ready to use.

LEMON ROSE

Strips of lemon peel are rolled into roses to garnish dinner plates and serving platters.

1 lemon (orange, turnip, or beet can also be used)
Paring knife
Toothpick
Salt

Cut off and discard the bulge at the stem end of the lemon (Figure 1). Start at the stem end and cut a continuous thin strip of peel about ¾-inch wide (Figure 2). For best results, use an up-and-down sawing motion when you cut. Avoid cutting into the pulp.

To roll the peel without splitting it, place it overnight in heavily salted water to soften. When the peel is soft and pliable, rinse in warm water. With the yellow side in and white part out, begin tightly rolling the strip from the stem end (Figure 3). Roll the first of the strip tightly, the rest loosely. Secure the end of the strip by pushing a toothpick through the side to a depth of ½ inch (Figure 4).

Now look at your rose. If it is too tight and symmetrical, remove the toothpick and loosen the last few turns. Replace the toothpick. If you are satisfied with the appearance, break off the portion of the toothpick that shows. Turn the rose on its side. Trim the bottom with the knife so that the rose will rest at an angle.

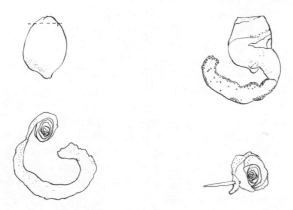

To Prepare in Advance. Finished roses can be kept indefinitely in the freezer. Place them in a container half-full of water and freeze. Then add enough water to cover the roses and freeze solid until needed. When ready for use, thaw overnight in the refrigerator or leave at room temperature until completely thawed.

SPIRAL TWIST

A spiral of orange peel is swirled into a graceful twist to garnish and lend balance to any plate.

    1 medium navel orange
    Large bamboo skewer
    Sharp paring knife
    Parsley
    Orange blossom

Cut off the top one third of the stem end of the orange. Push the skewer through the middle of the orange so that it sticks out the opposite end.

With a sawing motion, use the paring knife to cut twice around the orange, always keeping the knife blade in constant touch with the bamboo, to make a slice ¼-inch thick. Slice upward to free the peel. Repeat the process. One orange should provide about three spiral twists.

Place the twist on a flat surface. Lift up the tip of the spiral and twist it backward to form an elevated *S* shape. Tuck a small sprig of parsley into the hollow of one of the curves and nestle an orange blossom on top.

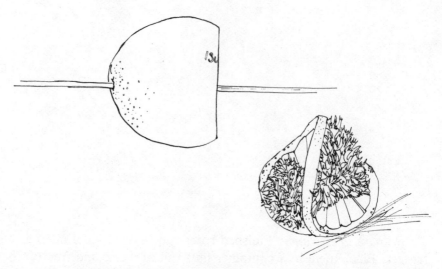

To Prepare in Advance. The spiral twists can be cut the night before your party and stored flat in an airtight plastic bag in the refrigerator. When ready to use, twist, decorate, and add to the platter.

MOLDING AND UNMOLDING

Unmolding without destroying your creation can be a problem. Working a knife along the inside of a mold to break the air suction is unsatisfactory, and placing the mold in hot water for a few seconds is inconvenient and messy. We have evolved a method that can be used for any cold molds. Do not use this method for molds to be used in the oven.

You will need a hammer, a ⅛-inch-diameter nail, a small rat-tail file, a piece of wood, a roll of masking tape, and about four minutes of your time. Pound the nail through the inside "top" of your mold and into the piece of wood. Discard the nail and the wood. Using a small rat-tail file, file off the rough, uneven edges on the outside of the mold (Figure 1). When ready to use the mold, cover the hole on the outside with a piece of heavy masking tape. (Transparent Scotch tape is not recommended.) Fill the mold with your preparation (see *Note*).

After the mold is chilled and you are ready to unmold, invert the mold on a serving plate, moistened with cold water to help center the food after unmolding. Remove the tape, thereby breaking the suction, and the food will pop out onto the plate. This should work every time. However, if the molded item fails to emerge, cover the outside of the mold for a few seconds with a warm, damp towel.

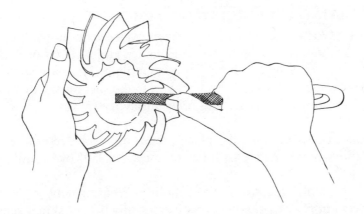

Note: To measure the capacity of a mold, fill it with water. Pour the water into a measuring cup. The amount of water will be the capacity of the mold.

ICE RINGS

For ice rings, any size ring mold can be used. Just be sure it will fit the punch bowl you plan to use. We use a 12-cup size because a ladle fits through the center of the ring for easy serving.

Place about ½ inch of *distilled* water in the ring mold. (Do not use ordinary tap water: The impurities and bubbles will cloud visibility and hide the garnish.) Freeze the ring in the bottom section of your freezer until a thin coating of ice forms on the surface. Crack the entire surface of the ice crust with the tip of a spoon to expose the water beneath. Working quickly, decoratively arrange your ice ring garnishes (mint leaves; lemon, orange, or cucumber slices; fern fronds; plastic holly; candied cherries, for example) in the water, making certain that each piece is partially submerged. Return the mold to the freezer until the water is solidly frozen, locking the garnish within the ice.

When this water is thoroughly frozen, add another inch of chilled distilled water. (Using chilled water prevents the first layer from melting and disarranging the garnish.) When the second layer of water is frozen, completely fill the mold with more chilled distilled water. When the ice mold is set and frozen, move it to the top section of your freezer. This will prevent it from overfreezing.

Some Tips: Don't make the ice mold more than 24 hours before serving; otherwise the water turns cloudy. Depending on its size, an ice ring usually lasts about 2 hours after it is placed in the punch.

TIMESAVING TECHNIQUES OR BASICS

In that last-minute rush to complete your menu preparations, the thought of having to stop to peel and mince garlic cloves or rinse and chop parsley may be too much to contemplate. Here are some timesaving techniques and basics to help you make short work of washing, peeling, toasting, chopping, and other unsavory chores.

Almonds. To toast almonds, place them one layer deep on a cookie sheet or in a pie pan and toast for 10 minutes in a 350° oven until golden.

Chiles. Hot chiles require special handling. Wearing rubber gloves is a wise precaution when handling them, especially if your skin is sensitive. Do not touch your face or eyes while working with any kind of chiles. If you do so, rinse the skin area thoroughly with water.

Garlic. Separate a whole head of garlic into cloves and peel. Press the cloves through a garlic press or mince in a dry food processor fitted with a steel blade. Transfer to a small jar suitable for refrigerator storage. Date the jar. Stir in 1 tablespoon vegetable oil to moisten the garlic and prevent its drying out. The purée will keep in the refrigerator up to one month. When you need garlic, use ¼ teaspoon of the purée for each medium clove called for.

Mushrooms. Purchase mushrooms that have closed gills and that feel moist. Refrigerate them unwashed in an open bag, loosely covered with a damp paper towel. Do not seal in a plastic bag or they will "sweat" and lose their freshness very quickly. Or, you can prepare them ahead of time by washing them quickly but gently under cold running water and drying them immediately with a towel. Never soak mushrooms; they absorb water like a sponge and will be soggy when cooked. Store as described. They will stay fresh and moist for 2 days.

Parsley. Rinse parsley under cold running water. Shake it dry and wrap in several layers of damp paper towels. The moist towels prevent "sweating." Refrigerate up to one week in a sealed plastic bag. For chopped parsley, place in a jar after chopping. Cover with a damp paper towel and seal. It will keep refrigerated up to one week and is convenient for last-minute garnishing.

Shallots. Mince shallots by hand or in a food processor fitted with a steel blade. Coat with oil and store as directed for garlic. Date the jar.

When prepared this way, shallots will keep in the refrigerator up to ten days. Use 1 tablespoon of minced shallots per each large shallot called for in a recipe.

Tomatoes. To peel a tomato, dip it into boiling water for 30 seconds. Cut out the stem end and peel. The skin will slip right off. (It is not necessary to skin the tomato immediately after dipping but can be refrigerated until needed.)

Zest. The finer outer skin of citrus fruit called the *zest* can be removed in several ways: Use a very fine grater, taking care not to remove the bitter white pitch with the peel; or use a vegetable peeler to remove just the outermost skin and then chop it; or, easiest of all, use a gadget called a zester which can be purchased at gourmet cookware shops, remove all the zest, freeze the excess for future use.

INDEX